CONTENTS

Library of Congress Cataloging-in-Publication Data

Names: Rogers, Daniel E., 1962- author.
Title: Battleship *Alabama* / Daniel Rogers.
Other titles: Naval history 1042-1920
Description: Annapolis, MD : Naval Institute Press, [2022] | Series: Naval
   history special edition | Title from cover.
Identifiers: LCCN 2022022405 | ISBN 9781591146988 (paperback)
Subjects: LCSH: Alabama (Battleship : BB-60) | World War, 1939-1945--Naval
   operations, American. | Battleships--United States--History--20th
   century. | BISAC: HISTORY / Military / Naval | HISTORY / Wars &
   Conflicts / World War II / General
Classification: LCC D774.A4 R64 2022 | DDC 940.54/5973--dc23/eng/20220510
LC record available at https://lccn.loc.gov/2022022405

T0037711

INTRODUCTION

Newspapers across the United States carried a brief story in early February 1940. "Keel Laid for 35,000 Ton Battleship," read the headline in the *Honolulu Star-Bulletin*. In Montgomery, Alabama, the *Advertiser* ran an especially detailed account, for this battleship was to be named for the state of Alabama itself. It noted that "the Navy has a long established custom of naming battleships for the states of the Union." The forthcoming USS *Alabama* would be neither the first warship, nor the last, to be named for the 22nd state of the Union (see "*Alabama*–A Great Name in Fighting Ships," on page 11).

The estimated price at the time for this technological marvel was $69 million. Some later estimates reached $77 million. The staggering cost, the equivalent of at least $1.2 billion today, would be borne by a nation not fully recovered from the Great Depression. The financial sacrifice revealed the urgency with which the U.S. government was approaching the question of rearmament in the late 1930s. A resurgent Nazi Germany and a menacing Imperial Japan were constructing and commissioning battleships whose weapons, armor, and propulsion systems leapfrogged those of the battleships of the U.S. fleet, which had all been commissioned before, during, or just after World War I—a quarter of a century earlier.

Alabama was one of ten "fast battleships" that the U.S. Navy commissioned between 1941 and 1944 (see the table "U.S. Fast Battleships of World War II" on page 14). They were the latest and most sophisticated in a long line of ships that many scholars of naval warfare trace back to the seventeenth century.

VITAL FACTS AND SPECIFICATIONS

Builder	Norfolk Navy Yard, Virginia
Keel laid down	1 February 1940
Launched	16 February 1942
Sponsor	Henrietta McCormick Hill (wife of Alabama U.S. senator J. Lister Hill)
Commissioned	16 August 1942
Delivered	10 November 1942
Decommissioned	9 January 1947
Stricken from Naval Vessel Register	1 June 1962
Opened as museum in Mobile	9 January 1965
Design displacement	35,000 tons
Full displacement	44,374 tons
Length overall	680 feet
Beam	108 feet, 2 inches
Maximum navigational draft	36 feet
Maximum speed	27.5 knots
Range	15,000 nautical miles at 15 knots
Crew	approximately 2,500 during World War II
Shaft horsepower (total)	130,000 hp
Armament (museum configuration)	9 x 16-inch/45-caliber guns in 3 triple turrets
	20 x 5-inch/38-caliber guns in 10 double mounts
	48 x 40-mm guns in 12 quadruple mounts
	52 x 20-mm guns
Aircraft	3 x Vought OS2U Kingfisher floatplanes (1942–45); Curtiss SC Seahawk floatplanes (1945)

Henrietta McCormick Hill, wife of Alabama U.S. senator Lister Hill, served as the sponsor of *Alabama* at her launching in February 1942. (NHHC)

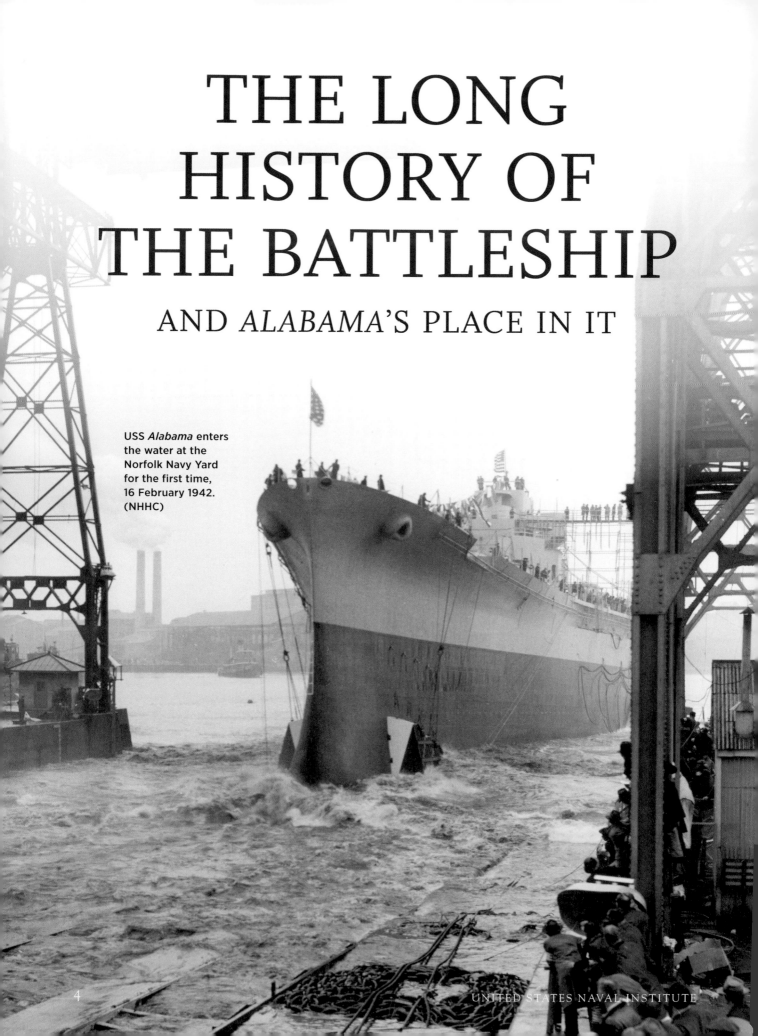

THE LONG HISTORY OF THE BATTLESHIP

AND *ALABAMA'S* PLACE IN IT

USS *Alabama* enters the water at the Norfolk Navy Yard for the first time, 16 February 1942. (NHHC)

The "battleship" of the 20th century can trace its origins to the "ship of the line" of the 17th century. Ships of the line were designed to fight as part of a group, forming a column when firing their cannons. Under the command of a single admiral, they would fire broadsides at a similar line of enemy warships, which would be, by today's standards, exceedingly close. The first ships of the line were constructed of wood, such as oak, and propelled by sails on masts. The largest among them carried as many as one hundred guns. For nearly two centuries these ships would retain their basic characteristics and capabilities.

But beginning in the mid-19th century, the Industrial Revolution dramatically altered these ships of the line into warships that were far faster, better protected, and deadlier. Rapid technological advances in metallurgy, propulsion, explosives, optics, analog computing, and (ultimately) radar enabled the great navies of the world to construct expensive, heavily armored, $69 million steam-propelled ships that could fire heavy ordnance accurately far over the horizon.

The first battleships in the modern sense were laid down in the 1870s and are referred to as "predreadnoughts," since they operated in the decades before the revolutionary HMS *Dreadnought* was launched in 1906. They replaced ironclad warships of the previous decades with an all-steel construction protected by thick armor. They were propelled by coal-fired boilers producing steam that drove multiple-expansion engines that, in turn, spun propellers ("screws"). They had a mixture of large-, medium-, and small-caliber weapons for fending off a variety of perceived threats.

After the War of 1812, the U.S. Navy had started building ships of the line, among them USS *Franklin* and USS *Columbus*. But owing to their expense and complexity and the lack of sufficient political will to finance a great navy, the U.S. Navy could deploy few of these warships for the rest of the nineteenth century. When Argentina, Brazil, and Chile were constructing battleships of their own in the 1880s, the United States, alarmed, fully rejoined what could now be called the "battleship club" by launching USS *Texas* in 1892. *Texas*, though, was originally authorized as an "armor-clad" vessel rather than a "battleship." The first battleship designated as such and regarded as on a par with European battleships of the time was USS *Indiana* (BB-1), commissioned in 1895. The U.S. pre-dreadnoughts included the first battleship named for the state of Alabama: BB-8, commissioned in 1900 and served through World War I and until 1921, when she was sunk as a target by the nascent U.S. Army Air Service.

The first battleship USS *Alabama* (BB-8), after being stricken from the Naval Vessel Register and while being used as a target in the Chesapeake Bay by the U.S. Army Air Service in September 1921. (NHHC)

THE DREADNOUGHT REVOLUTION

In 1906, Britain's Royal Navy commissioned HMS *Dreadnought*, inaugurating a new era in battleships. *Dreadnought* and ships based on her design that followed were long-range warships intended to assert Britain's interests powerfully around the globe. The novelties of *Dreadnought* included an "all-big-gun" design; the many smaller guns that had armed older ships were replaced by an array of ten 12-inch guns in five turrets. Her faster top speed, 21 knots, was made possible by steam turbine engines, the first to be employed on battleships. She was also specifically designed to take advantage of fire-control systems under development that would become available in 1912. When they arrived, these systems marked the advent of the era in which battleship fire was centrally directed and aided by analog computers that dramatically increased the ranges at which battleships could deliver accurate fire from their main batteries.

Before the dreadnought era, guns had been fired "locally"—that is, controlled by an officer at the gun itself attempting to aim ("lay") it to hit the target. With the installation of central fire-control systems on board the dreadnoughts, decisions about laying the guns and timing their firing were transferred to gunnery officers in a central location. The gunnery officers were aided by men in fire-control directors located in towers high above the guns for maximum visibility. But most importantly, fire control came to rely on the analog computers that were developed to take into account rapidly the variables resulting from movement on the sea that affect both the firing ship and, usually, its target as well.

As the guns grew larger, these variables took on increasing importance because of the increased time the larger shells might be in flight. Among these variables were the initial velocity of the projectile as it left the barrel; wind speed and direction; humidity (air density); the speed, heading, pitching, and rolling of the firing ship; the bearing, heading, speed, and range (distance away) of the target ship; and even the rotation of the earth beneath the projectile during the many seconds it flies through the air. Refinements in central fire-control systems continued throughout the remainder of the battleship era.

The U.S. Navy, along with the navies of all the other great powers of the era, attempted to keep pace with the innovations of the British dreadnoughts. The battleships of the *South Carolina*–class (BB-26) were the first American dreadnoughts. They

HMS *Dreadnought*, commissioned in 1906, changed the world's understanding of the battleship. (NHHC)

USS *South Carolina* and her
innovative superfiring main-
battery turrets. (U.S. Navy)

pioneered the U.S. Navy's superfiring turrets: all the rotating main gun turrets were placed on the ships' centerlines, but turrets closer to the center of the ship would be mounted higher above the waterline, enabling turrets on the same end of the ship to fire down the ship's centerline at the same time and all turrets to fire broadsides together. So successful was this design that all the navies of the world gravitated toward it.

The world's battleships were transitioning from burning coal to oil in order to generate the steam to spin their turbines and hence turn their propellers. The U.S. Navy began the conversion in the aftermath of the Spanish-American War, during which its ships had sometimes struggled in campaigns in the western Pacific to refill their coal bunkers. Taking on coal was a long, labor-intensive practice compared to fueling with oil, which in due time would be delivered in combat scenarios by means of midocean refueling from "oilers," specially fitted tankers.

Oil had other advantages for the U.S. fleet. It produced more energy per pound than coal. The United States was beginning to develop significant domestic petroleum fields for the use of the Navy. Finally, burning coal produced thicker smoke and produced unhealthy ash residue breathed by the many men required to stoke the boilers. In 1916, the U.S. Navy commissioned its first two oil-fired battleships, USS *Nevada* (BB-36) and USS *Oklahoma* (BB-37), and began converting coal-fired ships to petroleum.

THE SUPERDREADNOUGHTS

What *Dreadnought* had begun could not be stopped: the navies of the world continued to experiment with and deploy battleships with heavier main guns, more armored protection, more powerful engines (hence greater speed), increased displacement, and more advanced fire-control systems. Within a few years, therefore, the dreadnought era transitioned into the final period of battleship design, that of the "superdreadnought." It came to an end only during World War II, finding its ultimate expression in the two Japanese battleships of the *Yamato*-class. Whereas in 1906 *Dreadnought* had displaced about 18,000 tons, *Yamato* would displace 65,000. *Dreadnought* had ten 12-inch main guns; *Yamato* had nine of 18.1 inches. *Yamato*'s top speed of 27 knots was over 28 percent faster than *Dreadnought*'s 21 knots. Yet the superlative battleships in terms of combat effectiveness were the last ten battleships of the U.S. Navy, including USS *Alabama*. Fire-control systems aided by radar and linked to the most sophisticated computing instruments of the day gave them a decisive edge.

THE FAST BATTLESHIP ERA IN THE U.S. NAVY

It was during this period of a dizzying pace of innovation and improvement that the second battleship named USS *Alabama* (BB-60) was conceived. Her precise characteristics and capabilities were very much products of the political, diplomatic, economic, and technological context of the 1930s and early 1940s. She was one of ten "fast battleships" commissioned by the United States between 1941 and 1944.

These ten were the first battleships the United States had authorized since the end of World War I, twenty years earlier. Weary of the expense of trying to cope with each new improvement in battleship design, the five leading naval powers had joined together in the Washington Naval Treaty of 1922 to put a stop to new battleships for ten years and suspend the construction of most battleships then being built. These five powers—the British Empire, France, Italy, Japan, and the United States—also agreed to limits both on the total displacement tonnage of their battleships and to a 35,000-ton limit on any individual hull. Great Britain and the United States accepted a total limit on battleships of 525,000 tons; Japan, 315,000 tons; and France and Italy, 175,000 tons (or, respectively, 15, 9, and 5 battleships displacing 35,000 tons each).

The largest gun allowed on any battleship was to be 16 inches in diameter. Total aircraft carrier tonnage and the size of any individual carrier were also capped by the treaty, and smaller warships were limited in displacement to 10,000 tons and in armament to 8-inch guns. Battleships and aircraft carriers could not be replaced until twenty years after completion. Under these terms, the earliest the United States was free to construct a new battleship was 1934. Since this opportunity came during the depths of the Great Depression and in a period without obvious foreign danger, it was passed over. In any event, a second international agreement, the London Naval Treaty of 1930, had extended the moratorium on new ship construction to 1936 at the earliest.

In 1936, Japan, which had begun a campaign of aggression against China five years earlier, decided to

USS *Missouri* (BB-63), one of the four *Iowa*-class battleships, in 1945. (U.S. Navy)

withdraw from talks in London about continuing the Washington Treaty process and its limitations. These talks produced the Second London Naval Treaty, according to which the largest, or "capital," ships were still limited to 35,000 tons, but the biggest guns of new ships could be only 14 inches in diameter. An "escalator clause," though, permitted 16-inch guns if Japan (or Italy, which had also withdrawn from the talks) refused to rejoin the process and agree to the new limits by April 1, 1937. These two future partners in the "Axis" of World War II would, in fact, no longer participate.

By 1937, the U.S. Navy had already begun designing and planning for its first new battleship since the commissioning of USS *West Virginia* (BB-48) in 1923. This was to be the lead ship of a two-member class, USS *North Carolina* (BB-55). Several major constraints were in play in the design of these first two new battleships:

- How much the U.S. Congress was willing to finance

- The London Naval Treaties

- The prevailing principle in battleship design that any battleship be able to withstand fire from main batteries up to the size of its own

- The need for "beam" (width) and draft small enough to squeeze through the 110-foot-wide Panama Canal and enter U.S. naval bases and most major ports

- The desire to make new battleships fast enough to keep pace with 26-knot battleships that U.S. intelligence estimated Japan and other navies were constructing.

The *North Carolina*–class was, accordingly, at first designed to carry 14-inch guns and armor to withstand fire from 14-inch guns. Although it proved possible to switch the guns to 16 inches in response to Japanese and Italian refusal to abide by the smaller limits, it was too late to redesign the armor and still start construction of the ships on time. Thus *North Carolina* and her sister ship, USS *Washington* (BB-56), were underprotected by the standards of the time, but this deficiency was to have little practical effect during the ships' battles in World War II.

The next group of four battleships to be laid down, those of the *South Dakota*–class (including *Alabama*), would not suffer from this apparent mismatch between gun size and armor protection; their design began after the decision had been made to escalate the main-gun size to 16 inches. They bore many outward similarities to the *North Carolina*s but with two conspicuous differences: the *South Dakota*s had a single stack and were shorter overall (the *North Carolina*s 728 feet, the *South Dakota*s only 680). The *South Dakota*s' extra armor compelled the naval architects to shorten them in order to save overall weight. But the main and secondary-gun batteries were identical (except on *South Dakota* herself; see "Antiaircraft Defense" below).

Even as the *South Dakota*s were being constructed, a third class of fast battleship was being laid down, the four *Iowa*s: USS *Iowa* (BB-61); USS *New Jersey* (BB-62); USS *Missouri* (BB-63); and USS *Wisconsin* (BB-64). (*Wisconsin* was to be the last U.S. battleship ever commissioned and the last to fire her main guns in combat, in 1991). The *Iowa*s were heavier (45,000 tons), longer (887 feet), and faster (33 knots) than either the *North Carolina*s or *South Dakota*s and represented the

culmination of U.S. battleship technology—technology that made the *Iowa*s, *South Dakota*s, and *North Carolina*s, the ten "fast battleships" (one of them *Alabama*), the most effective such ships the world would ever know.

The life of *Alabama* herself can be considered to have begun with the authorization by the U.S. Congress of the *South Dakota*–class battleships, in two bills of 1934 and 1937. President Franklin Roosevelt, who had been Assistant Secretary of the Navy from 1913 to 1920, remained keenly interested in the Navy, personally managed many of its affairs, and chose the names of the four *South Dakota*–class ships himself. *Alabama*'s keel would be laid down on 1 February 1940 at the Norfolk Navy Yard, but the massive expansion of the Navy under way at the time meant that several years would be necessary for her to be constructed, complete her trials, and enter active service. She was ready to be launched on 16 February 1942, shortly after U.S. entry into the war; her fitting out continued there until she was ready to be commissioned into service, on 16 August 1942, her official "birthday." She would carry up to 2,500 men at a time into combat over the next three years and never lose a man to enemy fire—her appreciative crew would call her "The Mighty A."

This special edition of *Naval History* is her story—one of serving her country well and faithfully for three years when its very existence was at stake, and then reminding all who would visit her over the decades in Mobile of the high price to be paid for freedom and independence.

The commissioning ceremony at the Norfolk Navy Yard, 16 August 1942. Notice the 40-mm gun tubs on the fantail are still empty. (NHHC)

ALABAMA

A GREAT NAME IN FIGHTING SHIPS

By Midshipman Ernest C. White, U.S. Navy, *Proceedings*, August 1942

ERNEST CANTRELL WHITE, 1921–2018, A 1942 GRADUATE OF THE U.S. NAVAL ACADEMY FROM HUNTSVILLE, ALABAMA, WENT ON TO SERVE ON BOARD USS LOUISVILLE IN WORLD WAR II AND RETIRE AT THE RANK OF COMMANDER IN 1968. THOUGH WRITING IN 1942 USING THE TERMINOLOGY OF HIS ERA, NOT OURS, MIDSHIPMAN WHITE PROVIDES A THOROUGH EXPLANATION OF THE ORIGINS AND HISTORY OF THE NAME THEN BEING GIVEN TO THE NAVY'S NEWEST BATTLESHIP.

It is February 16, 1942. At the Norfolk Navy Yard, hundreds of workers and high officials have gathered to witness the launching of the USS *Alabama*. Mrs. Lister Hill, wife of the junior senator from Alabama, anxiously awaits the signal to christen the powerful vessel as she starts down the ways. A few workmen hurriedly complete last-minute preparations. Everything is in readiness. Suddenly, the signal! A husky swing smashes a bottle of champagne across her bow! Bedlam breaks loose as neighboring ships salute the giant newcomer, and a mighty addition to the U.S. Fleet slides majestically down the ways. With her go the stirring traditions of a great navy—traditions built during peace and war—and with her go memories of the glorious part ships of her name have had in building those traditions.

Her name, itself, has a warlike origin. When the Spaniards settled along the Gulf Coast in 1541 they found a fierce, warlike Indian tribe called the Alibamons. From this date until they were finally suppressed in 1814, these Indians fought savagely against the advances of the white man. Although they were outnumbered by the Chickasaw and Choctaw Indians, their unceasing battle for their land caused it to become known as the Territory of the Alibamons. In 1817 it became the Territory of Alabama and was admitted to the Union in 1819.

Alabama was first adopted as a ship name following the Act of March 3, 1819, and has since been borne by six warships: a 74-gun ship of the line built in 1819, a steamer purchased in 1843, a gunboat bought during the Civil War, the CSS *Alabama*, a first-class battleship authorized in 1896, and a first-class battleship launched in 1942. Of these ships, the most

widely renowned is the CSS *Alabama*, but each of them has played, or will play, a great role in the history of the United States.

The first *Alabama* was laid down at the Portsmouth Navy Yard in 1817 and was originally intended to be a storeship. At this time, little interest was shown in the Navy, and work on her was delayed over a period of many years. Indeed, it is likely that she would never have been finished had it not been for the aid of the many political campaigns during the years she was under construction. Most of this period found her lying neglected in the shipyard. During political campaigns, however, interest was revived and prospective voters were employed as well-paid workmen. In this fashion, she spent 47 years in the shipyard at Portsmouth before she was finally launched on April 23, 1864. No other ship in history required so much time between the laying of her keel and her launching.

The superstitious sailors of her day may have considered it a bad omen that she spent so many years on the ways. It was, however, to prove only an indication of the many years of faithful service she was to have. After her launching in the last year of the Civil War, she was renamed the *New Hampshire* and served during the war both at sea and as storeship at Port Royal. After the Civil War she served as a receiving ship at Newport, and in 1895 was loaned to the New York Naval Militia. She served as a training ship there for several years and on November 30, 1904, her name was changed to the *Granite State*. As the *Granite State* she served as a training ship and was comparable for her day to our *Prairie State* of today. She remained on loan to the New York Naval Militia until August 19, 1921, when she was sold. Thus ended a period of 104 years' service in our Navy. During this time she was to be renamed twice and was to see four other ships of her name make history on the high seas.

By one of those strange quirks of fate, the original *Alabama* was not the first ship of this name to see wartime service. By an even stranger one, the first *Alabama* to see wartime service under the Stars and Stripes never actually served in the Navy at all. When the Mexican War began, the original *Alabama* was spending her 29th year on the stocks at the Portsmouth Navy Yard. As the enemy had no force to meet our ships on their element, no opportunities for brilliant naval engagements presented themselves. Ships for the transportation of troops and supplies were a vital need,

however, and it was as a troopship that an *Alabama* first saw service under the United States flag. This ship was purchased by the War Department and served under it throughout the war. In March of 1849, while she was lying unused at New Orleans, the *Alabama* was transferred to the Navy Department by the Secretary of War. Since her retention was expensive, she was immediately sold and passed from service without actually serving in the Navy.

When one thinks of the *Alabama* in connection with the Civil War, a picture of the great Confederate raider and her hopelessly gallant duel with the USS *Kearsarge* immediately comes to mind. Few people realize that three other ships of that name saw service during the War between the States as Union vessels. We have already seen the role played by the original *Alabama*

Alabama shortly after launching on 16 February 1942. (NHHC)

UNITED STATES NAVAL INSTITUTE

on the stage of history while she was masquerading as the *New Hampshire*. Others, too, were to adopt a stage name while engaged in the struggle against the state for which they were named. One of these, renamed the USS *Fox*, was purchased at a Key West prize court by the Navy Department. She was a small schooner but saw hot action in the lower Mississippi region. In April of 1863 she was chased into the Mississippi Sound. On September 12, 1863, she was burned and then taken by the Confederates. Her last curtain call was at Key West, Florida, on June 28, 1865, when she was sold at public auction.

The third *Alabama* to see service with the United States Navy during the Civil War was a wooden, side-wheel steamer which was commissioned at the New York Navy Yard in 1861. She carried a heavy armament for her type of vessel, and served in the North Atlantic Blockading Squadron for the duration of the war. She was taken out of commission at the Philadelphia Navy Yard on July 14, 1865, after a relatively uneventful career.

These three Union vessels are entirely obscured by the CSS *Alabama*, the greatest surface raider in the history of naval warfare. She was launched from the yard of Laird Brothers at Birkenhead near Liverpool, England, in 1862. She was not given a name, but was known by her yard number as *Number 290*. Despite orders for her seizure obtained by agents of the United States, she slipped down the Mersey on a "trial run" and put to sea. Although she was pursued by the USS *Tuscarora*, she soon vanished into the broad expanse of ocean and made good her escape.

Ten days later the *290*, or *Enrica* as she had been christened in the shipping articles, came to an anchor at the little-frequented island of Terceira in the Portuguese Azores. At this time she was commanded by English officers and manned by an English crew, so the Portuguese authorities readily extended the facilities of the port. Eight days later, on August 18, 1862, the bark *Agrippina* arrived from London and immediately began to transfer ammunition, coal, ship's stores, and the necessary guns for the *Enrica's* armament. Since both vessels were flying the British flag and were regularly entered on the customhouse books, Portuguese neutrality was satisfied, and the transfer was rapidly completed. A few days later, the British steamer *Bahama*, from Liverpool, arrived with the future officers of the *Enrica* on board. The three vessels took

to the open sea and made certain they were beyond Portuguese jurisdiction; the seamen were called aft, and Captain Raphael Semmes, C.S.N., stepped upon the quarterdeck and read his commission from Jefferson Davis. A starboard gun emphasized the change, as the British flag dropped to the deck and was replaced by the Confederate Stars and Bars. The Confederate States sloop-of-war *Alabama* was in commission. From this day, United States shipping was to be driven from the oceans to shrink beneath the protection of coastal guns as this ruthless destroyer combed the seas.

In the two years that she remained at sea, the *Alabama* was responsible for the almost complete destruction of U.S. commerce. Some 56 Union vessels, including whalers, cargo ships, mail steamers, and passenger vessels, fell into her hands. Since no neutral ports were open to prizes, and the *Alabama* had no Confederate port to which she could return, she was forced to destroy her prizes at sea. This increased the air of mystery that surrounded the Alabama and added to the panic that kept Union merchantmen near friendly ports.

In her two years of service, the *Alabama* met two United States warships in battle. Her first engagement was with the USS *Hatteras* off Galveston, Texas, on January 11, 1863. The two vessels were very nearly equal in strength. Although the *Alabama* had larger pivot guns, this was balanced in part by the fact that the *Hatteras* was 100 tons larger than was the *Alabama*. The crew of the *Hatteras* was 108 strong; that of the *Alabama* 110. This engagement was begun after it was quite dark and terminated 13 minutes later with the sinking of the *Hatteras*. A crew well trained in the handling of their ship, and her guns had sunk a comparable enemy with only one man wounded and negligible damage to their ship.

This engagement did much to heighten the legend of the *Alabama's* invincibility—a legend which was to be rudely shattered off Cherbourg the next year. On June 19, 1864, the *Alabama* steamed proudly out from Cherbourg to meet a greatly superior opponent, the USS *Kearsarge*. One hour and thirty minutes later, the bones of the greatest raider in naval warfare were lying on the wreck-strewn bottom of the English Channel.

The fifth *Alabama* to sail across the pages of history was launched by the Cramp Ship and Engine Building Company of Philadelphia in 1898. She was the first modern battleship to bear this name. Unlike her predecessors, she was destined for long service without ever engaging in battle. She accompanied the Great White Fleet on its 46,000-mile voyage begun in 1907, and was still on the active list when the United States entered the World War. She did not go overseas, however, but served as a training ship for seamen on the east coast of the United States. She was broken up and scrapped in accordance with the terms of the Washington Naval Conference of 1922.

Today, the sixth *Alabama* has slid proudly down the ways. Although she is unfinished, she has built in her the proud traditions of the United States Navy. As much a part of her as her engines or her guns are the noble words: "If the mast goes, we go with it!"; "We

U.S. Fast Battleships of World War II

"Fast battleship" was not an official U.S. Navy designation. It was used in practice to differentiate these ten battleships from the generations before them. While there were many other distinguishing characteristics, maximum speed was one of the most important. With speeds in excess of 27 knots, these battleships could do a much better job of keeping pace with the newer enemy battleships and the faster aircraft carriers, cruisers, and destroyers of their own navy.

Ship	Hull No.	Laid Down	Launched	Commissioned	Decommissioned
North Carolina	BB-55	27 Oct 1937	13 June 1940	9 April 1941	27 June 1947
Washington	BB-56	14 June 1938	1 June 1940	15 May 1941	27 June 1947
South Dakota	BB-57	5 July 1939	7 June 1941	20 March 1942	31 Jan 1947
Massachusetts	BB-59	20 July 1939	23 Sep 1941	12 May 1942	27 March 1947
Indiana	BB-58	20 Nov 1939	21 Nov 1941	30 April 1942	11 Sep 1947
Alabama	BB-60	1 Feb 1940	16 Feb 1942	16 Aug 1942	9 Jan 1947
Iowa	BB-61	27 June 1940	27 Aug 1942	22 Feb 1943	26 Oct 1990
New Jersey	BB-62	16 Sep 1940	7 Dec 1942	23 May 1943	8 Feb 1991
Missouri	BB-63	6 Jan 1941	29 Jan 1944	11 June 1944	31 March 1992
Wisconsin	BB-64	25 Jan 1941	7 Dec 1943	16 April 1944	30 Sep 1991

have met the enemy and they are ours!"; and "Don't give up the ship!" In her, too, is the fighting spirit of her predecessors—the Alibamons fighting gallantly to hold their land, the first *Alabama* with 104 years' service, and the CSS *Alabama*, the greatest raider of all time. Soon she will be completed, and will go forth to join the fleet. Her guns will speak, loudly, but with the voice of authority and not the braggart's boast. Her guns will speak "that this nation, under God, shall have a new birth of freedom—and that government of the people, by the people, for the people, shall not perish from the earth."

Some 43 years after White composed these words, the Navy commissioned yet another Alabama, one that White could never have imagined. As no new battleships were launched after 1943, the tradition of naming vessels for states was ultimately shifted to the ballistic-missile submarines of the Ohio-class. The latest Alabama, SSBN-731, was commissioned in 1985. She carries 24 Trident missiles tipped with nuclear warheads, along with torpedoes to counter threats from enemy vessels. She has been a vital part of the U.S. nuclear triad of bombers, land-based missiles, and submarines for decades, long surpassing all previous bearers of the state's name in years of frontline service.

Stricken from the Naval Vessel Register	Enemy-Inflicted Damage	Disposition
1 June 1960	Torpedo strike, Solomon Islands, 15 September 1942	Museum Ship, Wilmington, North Carolina
1 June 1960	None	Broken up
1 June 1962	1. Aerial bomb, Battle of the Santa Cruz Islands, 26 October 1942 2. Shellfire from Japanese ships, Naval Battle of Guadalcanal, 14–15 November 1942 3. Aerial bomb, Battle of the Philippine Sea, 19 June 1944	Broken up
1 June 1962	Struck by French shells during the Naval Battle of Casablanca, 8 Nov 1942	Museum ship, Fall River, Massachusetts
1 June 1962	None	Museum ship, Mobile, Alabama
17 March 2006	Struck by two Japanese projectiles from shore batteries at Mili Atoll, 18 March 1944	Museum ship, San Pedro, California
4 Jan 1999	None	Museum ship, Camden, New Jersey
12 Jan 1995	Struck by kamikaze aircraft near Okinawa, 11 April 1945	Museum ship, Pearl Harbor, Hawaii
17 March 2006	None	Museum ship, Norfolk, Virginia

MISUSE OF THE FAST BATTLESHIP IN WORLD WAR II

By Malcolm Muir Jr., *Proceedings*, February 1979

PROFESSOR MALCOLM MUIR JR. HAS WRITTEN NUMEROUS BOOKS AND ARTICLES ABOUT THE HISTORY OF THE U.S. NAVY IN GENERAL AND ITS FAST BATTLESHIPS OF THE WORLD WAR II ERA IN PARTICULAR. IN THIS ESSAY HE EXPLAINS THE GREAT POTENTIAL OF BATTLESHIPS SUCH AS USS ALABAMA AND ARGUES THAT NAVY LEADERS MAY NOT HAVE PUT THE VERSATILE AND POWERFUL NEW "BATTLEWAGONS" TO THEIR OPTIMAL USE DURING THE WAR.

During the 1930s, the battleship—not the carrier—formed the core of the rearmament program of the U.S. Navy. Congress authorized the construction of 17 fast (27 knots or more) battleships with extraordinary offensive and defensive powers. The projected cost was more than $1 billion, an unprecedented figure for peacetime. Eventually, seven of the vessels were canceled, but the ten ships which were completed formed a more powerful battle line than all the modern Axis battleships combined. Nonetheless, this potent American force saw relatively little action and failed to make a contribution commensurate with its power.

Part of the explanation can be found in the events of December 1941. The Pearl Harbor attack, and even more important, the sinking off Malaya of the new British battleship *Prince of Wales* caused the prestige of the big-gun ship to plummet. The idea that the type was hopelessly vulnerable gained widespread currency both inside and outside the Navy. Observers denounced battleships as "mammoths" and "sea dinosaurs," and the hypothesis that they were especially helpless against land-based air power became dogma for many officers. Cautious employment in both theaters became the order of the day. Indeed, when the first fast battleship reached the South Pacific, Rear Admiral Frank Jack Fletcher wondered what use he could make of it.

Yet by the end of 1942, the fast battleship had undergone a renaissance. This was in part attributable to the ability of the new ships to survive enemy air attacks. Armed with scores of modern antiaircraft guns, especially the 20-millimeter Oerlikon and 40-millimeter Bofors, two of the recently commissioned ships, the *North Carolina* (BB-55) and *South Dakota* (BB-57), not only held their own but rendered invaluable service in protecting carriers in the South Pacific in two separate actions. At the Battle of the Eastern Solomons in August 1942, the *North Carolina* destroyed seven planes without suffering significant damage. Two months later, the *South Dakota* turned in an even more dramatic performance while escorting the carrier *Enterprise* (CV-6) at the Battle of Santa Cruz Islands. Although the battleship was hit by a bomb, the *South Dakota*'s fighting capability remained unimpaired, and the antiaircraft gunners were credited with destroying 26 Japanese planes, the highest score ever recorded by a naval vessel in one action.

A second reassuring feature of the performance of the fast battleship was her ability to remain operational after serious damage, as the *North Carolina* demonstrated on 15 September 1942. A Japanese submarine torpedoed the ship just forward of the first turret. The blast tore a hole 32 feet long by 18 feet high in the ship's side. Nonetheless, the *North Carolina* maintained station in

A 32-foot-long hole in USS *North Carolina*'s side, from a torpedo hit on 15 September 1942. (U.S. Naval Institute photo archive)

the formation, even during radical maneuvers at speeds of 25 knots. Definitive repairs took two months, but the Bureau of Ships concluded, "We feel rather well satisfied at the performance which the *North Carolina* system gave."

Finally, in November, fast battleships gave convincing demonstrations in both Atlantic and Pacific Oceans that they were potent sea control weapons when presented with the opportunity. During the Allied invasion of North Africa, the *Massachusetts* (BB-59), on her shakedown cruise, provided key support by silencing the incomplete French battleship *Jean Bart* docked at Casablanca and by beating back a hasty French counterattack on U.S. troopships. The new American battleship helped sink or disable four Vichy destroyers and one light cruiser. A week later, in an even more crucial situation, the *South Dakota* and the *Washington* (BB-56), the principal ships in a task force commanded by Rear Admiral Willis A. Lee Jr., turned the tide at Guadalcanal by sinking the Japanese battleship *Kirishima*

Casablanca Harbor, showing the *Jean Bart* and the Lafond Basin to port of the battleship and the capsized hulk of the *Porthos*, victim of *Massachusetts*'s heavy guns, bottom left. (U.S. Navy)

The French liner *Porthos*, hit by a 16-inch shell intended for the *Jean Bart*, is capsized at dock. She had arrived in Casablanca early that morning carrying refugees from Dakar. (U.S. Navy)

UNITED STATES NAVAL INSTITUTE

in a night action and thereby saving American troops on the island from a devastating bombardment. Even more significant, the American victory convinced the Japanese command to evacuate its forces from the island. Samuel Eliot Morison later concluded that the Naval Battle of Guadalcanal "was decisive, not only in the struggle for that island, but in the Pacific War at large. . . . The conclusion of this great battle was marked by a definite shift of the Americans from the defensive to the offensive, and of the Japanese in the opposite direction."

The action also went far to retrieve the prestige of the battleship. Under Secretary of the Navy James Forrestal praised the ships for saving "Guadalcanal and the many thousands of gallant Americans in that bloodily contested jungle." Admiral Chester W. Nimitz, Commander-in-Chief of the Pacific Fleet, commented publicly: "The engagement justifies our faith in battleships." Admiral William F. Halsey, who had sent Lee's force into battle, jubilantly wrote to Nimitz, "I think we proved in Lee's night action that the day of the battleship is far from a thing of the past. How are all the experts going to comment now? They certainly inflicted terrific damage that night. The use we made of them defied all conventions: narrow waters, submarine menace, and destroyers at night. Despite that, the books, and the learned and ponderous words of the high brows, it worked."

Lee, in his action report, put his finger on the reason for the American victory. He admitted that his force was not superior to the Japanese in experience, skill, or training; the decisive margin resulted almost entirely, he said, from American radar. But, as many officers recognized, this was sufficient. Captain Glenn B. Davis of the *Washington* wrote to Admiral Nimitz: "Our radar is effective for accurate gunfire at long ranges at night. We should seek rather than avoid night action, opening at ranges as great as satisfactory solutions can be obtained." Other officers agreed, and articles appeared in the *Proceedings* applauding the venturous employment of battleships at Guadalcanal and calling for more of the same.

It is ironic, then, that Lee's fast battleships were involved in virtually no action during the next year, despite an increase in strength from four ships in January 1943 to six in August. His force could have been strengthened for offensive operations even earlier if the *South Dakota* and *Alabama* (BB-60) had not been sent to the North Atlantic, where they were fruitlessly engaged in operations with the British Home Fleet. The fast battleships which were in the Pacific spent much of 1943 riding at anchor at Noumea, New Caledonia. To relieve the tedium, some sailors guzzled cheap champagne bootlegged from Australia, while others hunted wild hogs ashore. The brunt of the fighting fell to the cruiser and destroyer forces in sharp actions such as Kula Gulf and Kolombangara. Some battleship officers felt that golden opportunities to employ their big guns were being missed. In the fall, Halsey on three occasions asked Nimitz for fast battleships to counter Japanese cruisers interfering with the invasion of Bougainville. Nimitz, however, declined to risk the ships against any lesser target than the Japanese main body, and this force, building its strength, stayed within the bastion of Truk.

With the arrival of the new *Essex*-class (CV-9) carriers in the fall of 1943, the U.S. Fifth Fleet, under the command of Vice Admiral Raymond Spruance, a specialist in the big gun, finally took the offensive in the Central Pacific. Spruance was anxious to force a showdown with the Japanese battle line, but he deployed his heavy ships in a surprising fashion. Short of cruisers and destroyers, he decided to split the fast battleships among the carrier task groups in order to provide both antiaircraft and surface support. In theory, the battle line would not be dissolved. Lee retained his position as Commander, Battleships Pacific, and his staff prepared signals and operations plans for the unit. If the Japanese challenged with their main fleet, Lee would pull his battleships out of the carrier task groups and form up for surface action. However, as long as the battleships steamed with the carriers, they were under the tactical orders of the carrier group commanders. This arrangement proved so successful from the standpoint of carrier warfare that it lasted until the end of the war.

Nonetheless, the continued assignment of the battleships to the carrier task groups condemned them to growing rusty in their surface role. Since Lee's ships were split among the carriers, he had little opportunity to assemble his commanders for conferences. Some of his chief subordinates were virtual strangers to him. Worse, his ships had almost no chance to exercise as a unit. By March 1944, Spruance had become quite concerned about the matter, and he tried to give Lee the opportunity to hold practice maneuvers. But with the rapid pace of operations in 1944 and 1945, the battle line rarely steamed as a unit. One officer who served with the fleet for the last six months of the war saw the battle line in formation just one time.

The night training of the battle line especially suffered. In contrast to the Japanese, the U.S. Navy had never been very proficient in nocturnal operations. Radar provided a partial equalizer, as the *Washington* had vividly demonstrated at Guadalcanal, but only practice could make the personnel comfortable with shiphandling in the darkness. And Lee's ships did not receive this practice. Spruance worried particularly about this, because the Japanese surface ships generally sought night battle. But in March 1944, when a Japanese challenge to Spruance's task force seemed imminent, an officer asked Lee how he would form the battle line in the event of a night attack. Lee replied, "Boy, the Jap fleet ain't intended to come out during this operation." Fortunately, it didn't.

In any case, the unreadiness of the battle line to function effectively in the dark was doubly unfortunate. For one thing, American fleet commanders were thereby deprived of their only strong weapon in a night battle, since carrier aircraft capabilities had not advanced to the surface ships' level. The 16-inch artillery laid by radar should have given task force commanders a powerful alternative to daytime aircraft carrier operations. The potential was certainly there; the fact that it remained undeveloped cost the fast battleships on two occasions the chance to deal crushing blows to the Imperial Japanese Navy.

The first opportunity came during the June 1944 invasion of Saipan, which the Japanese tried to counter by a sortie of their battle fleet. Spruance placed great reliance on Lee's ships to defeat the Japanese force and quickly sketched his intentions: "Our air will first knock out enemy carriers as operating carriers, then will attack enemy battleships and cruisers to slow or disable them. TG 58.7 [Lee's ships] will destroy enemy fleet either by fleet action if the enemy elects to fight or by sinking slowed or crippled ships if enemy retreats. Action against the retreating enemy must be pushed vigorously by all hands to ensure complete destruction of his fleet." Spruance turned over the responsibility for making more detailed plans to his two chief subordinates, Lee and Vice Admiral Marc Mitscher, the top carrier commander. The latter quickly calculated that if Japanese kept advancing, the American fleet, by moving to meet them, might force a surface engagement at night. He radioed to Lee, "Do you desire night engagement? It may be that we can make air contact late this afternoon and attack tonight. Otherwise we should retire to the eastward for tonight." Lee answered, "Do not repeat not believe we should seek night engagement. Possible advantage of radar more than offset by difficulties of communications and lack of fleet training in fleet tactics at night. Would press pursuit of damaged or fleeing enemy, however, at any time."

Spruance agreed with Lee that "the chances inherent in night fighting would neutralize American superiority," and the matter was dropped. Mitscher and his staff were "most disappointed." So were Nimitz's officers at Pearl Harbor. On board Lee's ships, some officers expressed surprise at their commander's decision. The gunnery officer of the *Iowa* (BB-61) later wrote, "I recall being surprised that the stated reason for not sending the fast battleships to look for the Japs in the Philippine Sea battle was lack of practice in night engagements. As far as my gunnery department was concerned, all our engagements, except for shore bombardments had been night shoots against Jap planes, and the main battery under full radar control couldn't have cared less whether it was day or night. I believe the other gunnery officers felt the same way." In any event, Spruance played a cautious hand during the battle, and the Japanese surface fleet escaped essentially unscathed, although the fleet air arm was virtually destroyed.

At Leyte Gulf four months later, the Imperial Japanese Navy a second time offered the opportunity for fleet action, but again the fast battleships missed the fight. This time the failure to engage in surface action was partly the result of Admiral Halsey's impulsiveness and partly the lack of night training. Japanese officers, in planning for this last-ditch effort, staked their hopes on their five fastest battleships, including the 18-inch-gunned *Yamato* and *Musashi*, under Vice Admiral Takeo Kurita. This force would have no chance of reaching the American transports unless Halsey's task force, which contained Lee's six battleships and Mitscher's carriers, could be lured away from its position outside the San Bernardino Strait. To accomplish this, the Japanese dangled Vice Admiral Jisaburo Ozawa's carriers, which lacked aviation components of any consequence, as bait to the north of Halsey.

The plan worked. As soon as Halsey discovered the whereabouts of the Japanese carriers, he took all his ships north, leaving not even a destroyer to watch the strait despite the news that Kurita's battleships were headed in that direction. Most of the officers in Halsey's force were taken aback. Mitscher's chief of staff, Commodore Arleigh Burke, proposed suggesting to Halsey that four of Lee's six battleships be detached to guard the strait, but Mitscher refused to forward the plan since Halsey had not asked for advice. On board the *Iowa*, top officers[,] including Rear Admiral Oscar Badger, "were unanimous in believing that a major error had been made." Lee was dismayed. His flag lieutenant, Guilliaem Aertsen, remembered, "We thought we could clean them up. . . . Lee . . . wanted to take his battleships and stand up and down in front of the straits. Lee's sole purpose was to take on the Jap fleet. It was a chance of a lifetime for the battleships." Lee was even willing to forgo air support if necessary. He felt so strongly that he sent his unsolicited views to Halsey, whose only reply was "Roger." Lee tried again when more information about Kurita's course was received, but to no avail.

To compound matters, Halsey did not make especially good time in approaching Ozawa's carriers, since the movement occurred at night. He delayed his fleet when he ordered Lee very early in the morning to form the battle line 10 miles ahead of the carriers. This entailed pulling the battleships out of formation in total darkness, and Lee insisted that his ships slow to 15 knots until the maneuver was completed. His chief of staff, Commodore Thomas P. Jeter, protested, "Admiral, what are you trying to do? We've got to get the ships together." But Lee insisted that higher speeds would be too dangerous. Because of these delays, "the next morning [American sailors] woke to a cloudless sky, a bright blue sea and gentle breezes, steaming North at 20 knots with battle flags flying," but with Ozawa still over the horizon.

Halsey soon received word that Kurita's heavy ships were assaulting American light forces covering the approaches to Leyte Gulf. After considerable hesitation and a query from Nimitz as to the whereabouts of the fast battleships, Halsey turned back. As Morison wrote, "It almost broke [Halsey's] heart to pull out Task Force 34 [Lee's ships] just as the battleships were on the point of reaching good gunfire-targets." In fact, Lee's ships were only 42 miles from Ozawa's force. Typically, Halsey took all six battleships south, but he had hesitated too

long, and the ships reached the strait three hours after Kurita had made his escape.

Thus, although the Japanese had taken a severe beating at the Battle of Leyte Gulf, most of their battle line had once more gotten away. These ships remained a thorn in the side of American planners for some time. Halsey futilely sent the *New Jersey* (BB-62) and *Iowa* all the way to the Indochina coast to try to catch two of the fugitives. When Spruance reassumed command of the fleet, he inherited this concern. At both Iwo Jima and Okinawa, he had to prepare for a possible surface action and was thus forced to cut back on the bombardment support that the fast battleships could have given the hard-pressed Marines. However, the Japanese fleet simply did not have the oil to mount a full-fledged effort, so the fast battleships spent the last days of the war fueling destroyers, providing antiaircraft support for the carriers, and shelling Japanese coastal cities.

Valuable as these duties might have been, they were clearly secondary to that of sea control, and in this, the carrier by the middle of the war had supplanted the battleship. Yet within range of her guns, the battleship remained unquestionably the most powerful type of warship, both offensively and defensively. The basic problem facing battleship commanders had been to bring their ships into contact with the enemy, and doing so invariably exposed the irreplaceable vessels to risks. Throughout the war, sailors ranging from ordinary bluejackets to high-ranking officers called for a more audacious employment of the big-gun ships, but the battleships were saved for the climactic fleet showdown that was narrowly missed on two occasions. Other navies fell victim to the same caution. The Japanese hoarded their most powerful battleships through the Guadalcanal campaign, even though they might well have turned the tide.

Nonetheless, the fact that a full-scale battle line action did not occur is no indictment of the entire fast battleship program. Surface ships were a significant threat during World War II. Of the 23 large combatant ships that the U.S. Navy lost, 9 succumbed to surface ship torpedoes or gunfire. Capital ships retained to the end a high degree of resistance to battle damage, as the Japanese battleships amply proved. The fast battleship remained a viable weapon in the sea control mission. Only bad luck and cautious employment kept her from a fuller vindication.

THE DESIGN AND FUNCTIONING OF THE *SOUTH DAKOTA* BATTLESHIPS

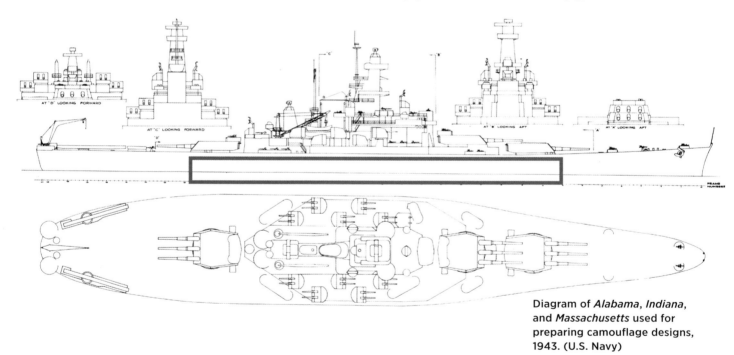

Diagram of *Alabama*, *Indiana*, and *Massachusetts* used for preparing camouflage designs, 1943. (U.S. Navy)

THE LAYOUT OF USS *ALABAMA* AND THE *SOUTH DAKOTA* CLASS

To simplify the task of understanding USS *Alabama* and her sister ships, it may be helpful to consider them as having three main sections:

THE ARMORED CITADEL starting with the second deck (i.e., the "floor" of the deck immediately below the main deck) and extending downward and running from the front of Turret 1 to rear of Turret 3 of the main battery. This is the portion of the ship containing the boilers, turbines, Combat Information Center, central station (which was capable of serving as an emergency bridge), damage control, plotting room, water distillation plant, main-battery guns, and powder magazines. A shell or bomb strike here could quickly disable the ship or impair some of her vital functions in combat. Thus, she was protected by heavy armor on all sides.

THE SUPERSTRUCTURE rising above the main deck. It might also be considered to extend one deck below the main deck to the level of the deck armor. With the exception of the conning tower, it was either lightly armored or unarmored. It contained officers' living quarters, the officers' galley and wardroom, some crew berthing and washrooms, the bridge and secondary bridge, the conning tower, the forward and aft main-battery fire directors, four secondary-battery fire directors, the engine exhaust stack, six 40-mm quadruple mounts and many 20-mm guns, the foremast and mainmast holding radio and radar antennas, and searchlights and signal flags. The ten mounts of the secondary 5-inch/38-caliber guns were located here on the first and second superstructure levels.

THE UNARMORED OR LIGHTLY ARMORED SECTIONS of the hull forward and aft of the armored citadel, running from the main deck down to the keel. On the deck itself, this area included 40-mm and 20-mm positions, the catapults for spotter planes, the crane to retrieve the spotter planes, the planes themselves, whaleboats, lifeboats, and a paravane for minesweeping work. The area in the stern below the main deck held the brig, crew quarters, crew messing areas, barbershop, laundry rooms, and storerooms. The bow area below the main deck contained crew berths and storage areas.

ARMOR

One of the defining characteristics of battleships is their heavy armor, often simply called the *protection*. It is designed to defend vital spaces from catastrophic damage from enemy fire or bombs. The price of this protection is an increase in the weight (displacement) of the ship and the consequent need to provide more power to propel her through the water at the desired speed. In the era of the naval limitation treaties, when USS *Alabama* was constructed, the enhanced protection forced her designers to struggle to keep the new battleships of the *North Carolina* and *South Dakota*–classes within the 35,000-ton maximum.

Since the beginning of the superdreadnought era in the second decade of the 20th century, the U.S. Navy had largely adhered to the principle known as "all or nothing" in the protection of its battleships. Rather than attempt to shield all areas of the ship

with thinner armor spread out more widely, the central area of the ship below the main deck, often referred to as "the citadel," would receive all the heavy armor, and the forward and aft sections little or no armored protection. The central area of the ship contained the power plant, the Combat Information Center, the plotting room, and the damage control station. In addition, each of the main gun turrets required heavy armored protection, because of the danger that an exploding shell or bomb could penetrate the turrets and ignite shells and the magazines holding the powder bags. Such a penetrating bomb dropped from an airplane, for instance, likely led to the detonation of one of the magazines of USS *Arizona* (BB-39) at Pearl Harbor on 7 December 1941.

Battleships were intended to steam in the company of other friendly battleships and to be prepared to take on groups of enemy battleships as one unit. The riskiest scenario under these circumstances was engaging battleships with the same-sized main guns, since such battleships were likely to be approximately as fast and therefore difficult to evade if the situation called for withdrawal.

Thus the armored protection on U.S. battleships, including *Alabama*'s class, was usually designed to protect against the widest variety of shell hits from similar-sized main guns. The *South Dakota*s, carrying 16-inch main guns, would be constructed with armor designed to defend against 16-inch shells from enemy battleships. Their design increased the armor protection over that on the preceding *North Carolina*–class without seriously compromising the ships' maximum speed by cramming the vital portions of the ships into shorter but better-protected armored citadels and by decreasing the overall length of the ships, thus saving weight.

Armor need not be the same thickness in every location in order to provide acceptable protection. Naval gunfire falls at target ships in relatively predictable arcs, depending on the distance from which it is fired. The most likely deadly impact would be on the side of the ship in the citadel area, or in one of the turrets or barbettes that surround the turrets. "Plunging fire" might also strike the deck, of course, as could bombs dropped from enemy dive-bombers. Thus the deck would need substantial armor as well. Indeed, as the war progressed the danger from enemy dive-bombers outweighed the danger from hostile battleships, and it became clear that there would be no adequate means of protecting battleships from dive-bombers other than to prevent their approach in the first place. As that role fell to aircraft carriers, the battleship became an increasingly dubious long-term bet for the world's navies.

Belt Armor

Alabama and the other battleships of the *South Dakota*–class had around the side of the armored citadel belt armor that measured 12.2 inches thick at the top (mounted on 7/8-inch "special treatment steel," or STS, backing plates). The belt armor ran down the sides of the ship, angled inward 19 degrees from the vertical to provide increased resistance to penetration. This angling gave the armored belt the equivalent protection of 17.3 inches of perfectly vertical plates. As the lower belt continued toward the bottom, it decreased in thickness, tapering down to one inch, since much of the force of projectiles passing through water would have been dissipated by the time they reached the bottom of the ship.

The belt armor was not on the outside of the ship but, rather, internal. Tanks holding fuel and water were closer to the outer edge of the ship's hull, providing, in conjunction with some void spaces, further cushioning of the explosive impact of projectiles, torpedoes, or mine detonations. The bottom of the ship too was protected by a triple layer of tanks containing oil or water and void spaces.

Deck Armor

The horizontal deck armor consisted of four layers. On the ship's centerline at the magazines, the main-deck armor was just 1.5 inches; the second deck was a full 5.75 inches at the centerline (and 6.05 inches outboard); a splinter deck just below the second deck intended to catch exploding fragments was 5/8 inches; and the third deck was 0.3 inches on the centerline. On the third deck above the steering gear the armor was

6.2 inches thick, and over the steering-engine rooms it was 6.35 inches; the sides of these steering spaces were protected by 13.5-inch plates inclined, again, at 19 degrees from the vertical. At the forward and aft ends of the citadel, the armored bulkhead measured 11.3 inches.

Conning Tower

The conning tower and communication tube running down from the tower to the armored citadel had 16-inch armored sides, a 7.25-inch roof, and a 4-inch deck plate in the conning station itself.

Main-Battery Turrets and Secondary-Battery Mounts

The three main-battery turrets had 18 inches of armor on their face plates, 12 inches aft, 7.25 inches on top, and 9.5 inches on the sides. The barbette enclosing the turrets had 17.3 inches of armor on the sides, decreasing to 11.6 inches on the centerlines. The secondary batteries, less crucial to the ship's survivability, were far less heavily protected. The major protection for these 5-inch mounts was designed only to shield the occupants from aerial strafing; it was composed of 2-inch STS plates, with 2 inches of armor for their magazines below as well.

The only essential systems left unprotected were the rudders and propellers. Their omission is inevitable in ship design. The resulting vulnerability is well illustrated by the torpedo explosion near a propeller shaft that, damaging one of the rudders of the German battleship *Bismarck* in 1941, caused the ship to be stuck in a turn and thus unmaneuverable during combat. She was sunk nearly 13 hours later after having turned repeatedly in wide circles.

Overall, the armor worked well on the *South Dakota*–class, if it can be judged by the few times any of its member ships were struck during combat. *South Dakota* and *Massachusetts* were the only ones to be hit by enemy

Armor on the *South Dakota* class

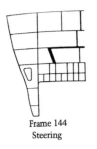

Frame 144
Steering

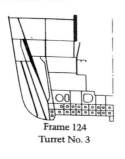

Frame 124
Turret No. 3

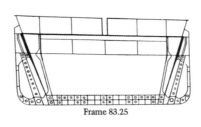

Frame 83.25

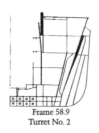

Frame 58.9
Turret No. 2

Frame 42
Turret No. 1

Frame 12.5

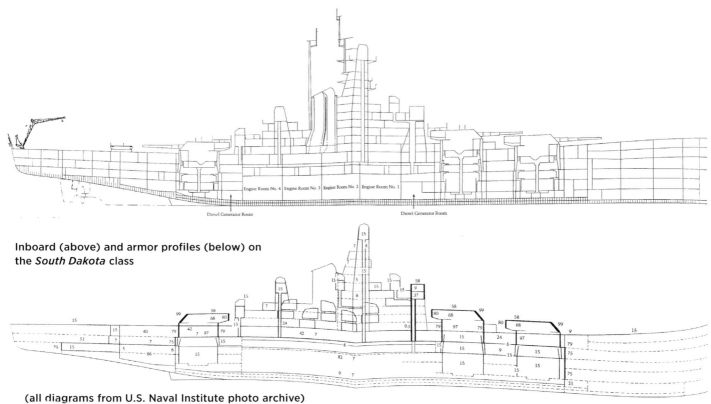

Inboard (above) and armor profiles (below) on the *South Dakota* class

(all diagrams from U.S. Naval Institute photo archive)

ARMOR THICKNESS

Key No.	Inches	Millimeters	Key No.	Inches	Millimeters	Key N.	Inches	Millimeters	Key No.	Inches	Millimeters
1	.25	6	26	2.80	71	51	6.20	157	76	11.50	292
2	.30	8	27	2.870	73	52	6.30	160	77	11.60	295
3	.375	10	28	2.925	74	53	6.60	168	78	11.70	297
4	.45	11	29	3.00	76	54	6.80	173	79	11.80	300
5	.50	13	30	3.20	81	55	7.00	187	80	12.00	305
6	.625	16	31	3.25	83	56	7.125	181	81	12.10	307
7	.750	19	32	3.30	84	57	7.20	183	82	12.20	310
8	.875	22	33	3.60	91	58	7.25	184	83	12.75	324
9	1.00	25	34	3.75	95	59	7.40	188	84	12.80	325
10	1.125	29	35	3.82	97	60	7.75	197	85	13.00	330
11	1.25	32	36	3.90	99	61	7.80	198	86	13.50	343
12	1.40	35	37	4.00	102	62	7.85	199	87	13.70	348
13	1.425	36	38	4.10	104	63	8.17	208	88	14.00	356
14	1.47	37	39	4.50	114	64	8.50	216	89	14.70	373
15	1.50	38	40	4.75	121	65	9.00	229	90	14.90	378
16	1.625	41	41	4.80	122	66	9.15	232	91	15.00	381
17	1.71	43	42	5.00	127	67	9.30	236	92	15.25	387
18	1.90	48	43	5.26	133	68	9.50	241	93	16.00	406
19	1.91	49	44	5.30	135	69	9.80	249	94	16.10	409
20	1.95	50	45	5.50	140	70	10.00	254	95	16.70	424
21	2.00	51	46	5.60	142	71	10.20	259	96	17.00	432
22	2.05	52	47	5.625	143	72	10.60	260	97	17.30	439
23	2.20	56	48	5.80	147	73	11.00	279	98	17.50	444
24	2.50	64	49	6.00	152	74	11.10	282	99	18.00	457
25	2.70	67	50	6.10	155	75	11.30	287	100	19.50	495
									101	21.30	541

projectiles or bombs during World War II. *South Dakota* was especially badly damaged during the Naval Battle of Guadalcanal and the Battle of the Philippine Sea but remained under her own power and capable of maneuver. The only time one of the *South Dakota*s risked foundering occurred not in combat but when *Indiana* turned in front of *Washington* during the Marshall Islands operations on 1 February 1944 and was struck forward of her starboard catapult. *Indiana* lost 200 feet of her armor plating but was able to limp back to the U.S. anchorage at Majuro Atoll for temporary repairs.

MAIN-BATTERY ARMAMENT

Alabama's main battery consisted of three rotating turrets, each holding three Mark 6, 16-inch/45-caliber guns. The guns rotated together with the turret, but each gun was mounted in its own sleeve, allowing it to be elevated or lowered independently of the others. The turrets could "train" (turn) the guns 4 degrees per second, while the guns could be elevated 12 degrees per second. The barrels' innermost liners were rifled with 96 twisting grooves that produced a complete rightward turn of a projectile once every 33 feet 4 inches as it was propelled toward the muzzle. In common with all rifled projectiles, the spinning 16-inch shells would move toward their targets with increased stability, thus making their point of impact more predictable.

The turret structure consisted of six horizontal levels, except for superfiring Turret 2, which had an extra stowage level since it extended higher above the main deck. Depending on the exact combat circumstances, a turret would be manned by a minimum of between 70 and 80 sailors. They worked in six main areas in or next to the turret:

- In the magazines, which completely surrounded the bottom of the turret
- In the powder-handling room on the lowest deck of the turret
- On the two projectile-handling rings midway up the turret from the powder-handling room
- On the electric deck

Turrets 1 and 2 of *Alabama*'s main 16-inch/45 batteries turned to starboard during practice firing in the North Atlantic. (U.S. Navy)

The rifling in the barrel of this gun on Turret 3 is visible in this photo from the shakedown period. (U.S. Navy)

- In the turret booth at the top of the turret, behind the gun pits

- In the gun pits themselves.

The magazines contained the cylindrical bags filled with the U.S. Navy's big-gun propellant, smokeless powder (SP). Rather than exploding as gunpowder does, the nitrocellulose-based SP burned extremely quickly. While this might seem like a distinction without a difference when viewing or hearing the mighty blast of the guns, using rapidly burning, rather than exploding, powder meant that pressures inside the barrels would be lower and the barrel life therefore longer.

Each of the powder bags was about 18 inches in diameter, 18 inches long, and weighed nearly 90 pounds, requiring strength and endurance among the crew lifting and moving them. The bags were made of silk, which would be burned nearly completely by the ignition of the powder. A red ignition pad was sewn to the end of each bag that was to be oriented toward the bottom of the barrel, so that it would ignite properly from the fire produced by the bag below (or, for the bag closest to the gun's breech, from the ignition of the primer). A full charge of propellant required six bags.

Because of their inherent volatility, the bags were loaded aboard ship in airtight canisters containing three bags and stored in the magazines, which were tightly sealed from the turrets and the rest of the ship. When the turrets were firing, powder bags would be passed one by one from men in the magazines through the powder doors of magazine scuttles. The bags would then be carried the short distance across the powder-handling deck to the powder car of a hoist that raised them to the gun room at the top of the turret.

The two main types of projectiles fired from the main battery were armor-piercing (AP), for enemy ships and hardened targets on land, and high capacity or high explosive (HE) for most shore bombardments. AP contained a far less potent explosive charge, since most of its damage would stem from penetrating the vital armored portions of an enemy ship or structure (see *Bluejacket Manual* section on ammunition, on page 30).

The projectiles were stored on two decks in the middle of the turret. These decks, known as the upper and lower projectile-handling decks, each consisted of two concentric circles. The outer of the two circles was stationary relative to the rest of the turret; there the 16-inch shells were stored, in an upright position, awaiting their hoisting up to the guns. When the turrets were firing, the projectiles would be moved over as needed to the inner ring, which could rotate either with or independently of the guns. The projectiles were moved across the inner ring's floor, using parbuckling equipment, into the projectile hoists along the outer perimeter of the inner ring. They would then ride the projectile hoist up to the gun room, nose first.

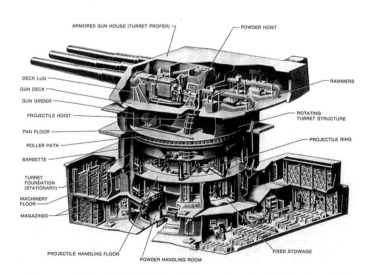

Diagram of the Mark 6, 16-inch/45 gun turret. (Public Domain)

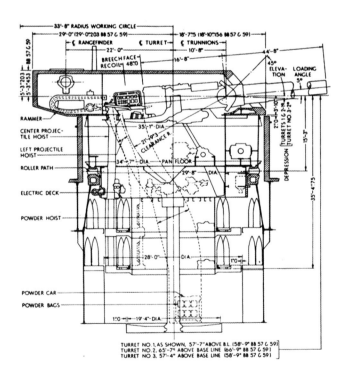

Diagram of Turret 1 of 16-inch/45 guns. (U.S. Navy)

Powder is loaded into the cars of the hoist that will elevate them to the breech of one of the 16-inch/45 guns. (U.S. Navy)

The powder-handling deck on Turret 2 of USS *Alabama* (museum configuration). Note the three powder bags in the hoist to the left and the powder canisters along the wall on the right. The portion of the turret to the left rotated; that on the right is attached to the stool supporting the turret and did not turn. (Daniel Rogers)

Turrets 1 and 2, 16-inch guns, firing during exercises. (NHHC)

Crew in a 16-inch/45 gun turret using parbuckling equipment to move one of the projectiles to the hoist that will elevate it to the gun room. (U.S. Navy)

loaded only with the barrel at an angle of elevation of five degrees above horizontal, meaning they had to be depressed back to that angle if they had been elevated higher (or, in very rare circumstances, elevated up that far if they had been firing level or even at a negative angle). The barrel was depressed automatically to five degrees each time the gun was fired, after the recoil cycle was complete.

Once the powder had been inserted and the breech closed and locked, the primer was inserted. The gun was now ready for firing. The turret officer, in a booth at the back of the turret, reported the ready status to the gunnery officer; normally, a sailor at the "stable vertical" in the plotting room would be the one who, when the time came, actually pulled the trigger firing the guns, shortly after sounding a warning siren to alert all nearby to prepare for the blast.

As the gun captain opened the breech again for the next round, a gas ejector expelled out through the muzzle any leftover gases or flaming fragments from the powder bags. A brief puff could be seen from the muzzles at this time.

The turret officer saw that the appropriate amount of powder and the proper kind of projectiles were moved from far below up to the guns. This officer would also be responsible, in the event of an emergency that disabled central fire control, for using sights and computer equipment in the turret booth to fire under local control. Thus men were stationed in the turret booth who could identify targets and sight the guns, although they almost never had to do so in combat.

EXCERPT FROM *THE BLUEJACKET'S MANUAL* (1944) ON AMMUNITION

For many generations, naval enlistees have received a copy of the U.S. Naval Institute's The Bluejacket's Manual *as their written introduction to the practices and customs of the U.S. Navy. In 1944, as USS* Alabama *was earning battle stars in the Pacific, this is how* The Bluejacket's Manual *explained Navy ordnance.*

Powder.—Except for saluting guns, impulse ammunition, and a few other special purposes, smokeless powder is used as a propelling charge in our Navy. It is in the form of cylindrical grains of various sizes for different guns. Powder for large guns is carefully stacked in silk bags which are sewed and laced to keep proper size and shape. These are stowed in magazines

The projectiles and powder would arrive via their separate hoists at the top of the turret on the gun deck. There were four men in each of the three gun pits in the turret; there was no need for them to move the shell by their own strength. First, the projectile would be gently lowered by a built-in apparatus at the top of its hoist into a cradle and spanning tray that extended to the breech of the gun. When the cradle was next to the breech, which the gun captain would have just opened, a rammer operator used his equipment to force the projectile quickly up into the barrel all the way to its firing position, where the rifling of the barrel began.

The rammer was extracted, leaving the breech open for the powder bags. Two of the men inserted the bags in the cradle one by one, and when all six bags were in the cradle, they were introduced into the barrel by the rammer operator—much more gently than the projectile had been, since over-ramming could lead to a catastrophic detonation with the breech open. The 16-inch guns, unlike the 5-inch batteries, could be in airtight metal tanks. A charge for any large gun is made up of one or more powder bags. A 5-inch gun uses one bag, a 16-inch gun uses four. At the base of the bag a black powder ignition charge is secured. It is ignited by the primer and in turn ignites the smokeless powder. This end of the bag is painted red and it is always placed toward the breech. Failure to put the red end toward the breech will cause hangfire and miss fire.

In fixed and semi-fixed ammunition the powder is contained in the cartridge case.

Among the other explosives used by our Navy is TNT, a high explosive. TNT is used for bursting charges such as the charge in the war head of a torpedo or in the projectile of a high explosive shell. It is also used in depth charges and mines which are exploded on contact or by pressure.

Projectiles.—*Armor-piercing projectile.*—The armor it will penetrate depends on the velocity of the projectile. It is cylindrical in shape with a solid pointed head. A soft steel cylindrical cap is fitted on the point of the armor-piercing projectile. When it strikes armor, the first shock bends the hard plate in while the projectile pierces its own cap. Its hard point then strikes the hard surface of armor. When the armor is bent nearly to its breaking point, the projectile enters easily.

Common projectile.—Thinner walls, thus allowing a larger space for the bursting charge.

Target practice projectile.—Same weight, size and shape as the common projectile, but made of much cheaper materials. It is filled with sand instead of a bursting charge to give proper weight.

Non-ricochet projectile.—Flat nosed with a large bursting charge; used against submarines.

Shrapnel projectile.—Cylindrical in shape with a round head. It is made of cast steel and has a small bursting charge and thin walls, its cavity being filled with a large number of small balls about 1/2 inch in diameter, packed in rosin or sulphur. Used against personnel or aircraft, shrapnel is set to burst in front of target.

Illuminating projectile.—Fitted with a time fuse which, when exploded, releases and ignites a large charge of slowly burning pyrotechnic material giving off a bright light. A parachute is used to suspend the illuminate.

Rotating band.—A copper band is secured in an undercut score around the projectile near the base. When the gun is fired, the lands of the rifling cut into the soft metal band causing the projectile to turn in the bore. The rotating band prevents the escape of powder gases past the projectile and centers its rear end in the bore of the gun.

Parts of the projectile.—

Nose; small end of the shell.

Base; large end.

MARKINGS OF PROJECTILES

Armor piercing	black
Common and black powder	slate
Shrapnel	white
Target practice	unpainted
Explosive D	yellow
Class B and cast TXT	dark green
Illuminating	blue with white star

Bourrelet; machine bearing surface near the forward end of the shell. It assists the rotating band in steadying the projectile as it moves out of the gun.

Tracers; a device fitted to the projectile to make it possible for the eye to follow it either in daylight or at night.

Primers.—Primers ignite the powder in the firing charge of a gun. Combination percussion and electrical primers are used for all heavy and intermediate guns. Percussion primers are used in 3-inch guns and under. The primer stock is made of bronze and is cylindrical in shape, the diameter of the base being about 6/10 of an inch and the length of the primer 2 inches. When a gun is fired by percussion, the firing pin strikes the base of the plunger which in turn strikes the fulminate of mercury cap, which fires the primer's charge igniting the firing charge. With an electric primer the current passes from the firing pin through the plunger, plunger cap, and a short platinum wire with a wisp of gun cotton around it called a bridge. The current heats the wire, ignites the gun cotton and powder, and thus fires the primer.

Fuses.—A fuse is used to explode the bursting charge in a projectile. The rotation of the projectile caused by the rifling of the gun makes a locking bolt fly out, arming the fuse. When the projectile strikes, the plunger flies forward and explodes the cap, which in turn ignites the black powder in the forward end of the fuse and finally the bursting charge of the shell. There are also time fuses which can be set to expose varying lengths of a train of powder, thus varying the time of explosion.

In antiaircraft fire the projectiles are fused in order to explode the projectile at a predetermined range. A fuse-setting mechanism is provided with each antiaircraft gun mount.

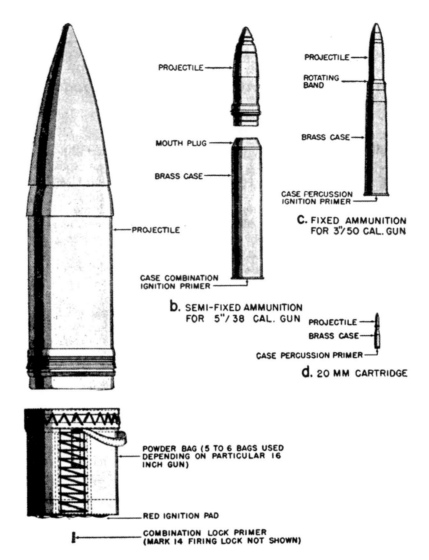

PROJECTILE

PROJECTILE

ROTATING BAND

MOUTH PLUG

BRASS CASE

BRASS CASE

CASE PERCUSSION IGNITION PRIMER

c. FIXED AMMUNITION FOR 3"/50 CAL. GUN

PROJECTILE

CASE COMBINATION IGNITION PRIMER

b. SEMI-FIXED AMMUNITION FOR 5"/38 CAL. GUN

PROJECTILE
BRASS CASE
CASE PERCUSSION PRIMER

d. 20 MM CARTRIDGE

POWDER BAG (5 TO 6 BAGS USED DEPENDING ON PARTICULAR 16 INCH GUN)

RED IGNITION PAD

COMBINATION LOCK PRIMER (MARK 14 FIRING LOCK NOT SHOWN)

a. BAG AMMUNITION FOR 16" GUN

MARKING OF PROJECTILES

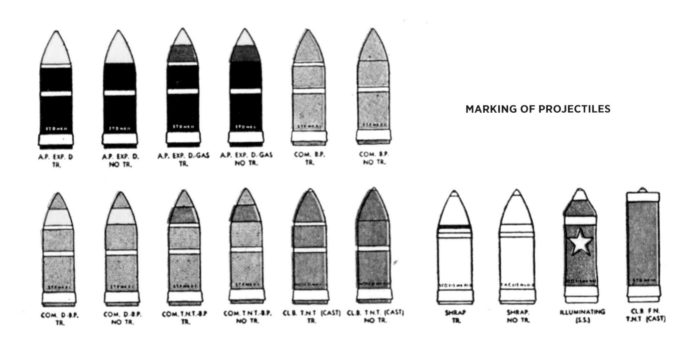

| A.P. EXP. D TR. | A.P. EXP. D. NO TR. | A.P. EXP. D. GAS TR. | A.P. EXP. D. GAS NO TR. | COM. B.P. TR. | COM. B.P. NO TR. | | | |

| COM. D-B.P. TR. | COM. D-B.P. NO TR. | COM. T.N.T.-B.P. TR. | COM. T.N.T.-B.P. NO TR. | CI.B. T.N.T (CAST) TR. | CI.B. T.N.T. (CAST) NO TR. | SHRAP. TR. | SHRAP. NO TR. | ILLUMINATING (S.S.) | CI.B. F.N. T.N.T (CAST) |

TYPES OF PROJECTILE

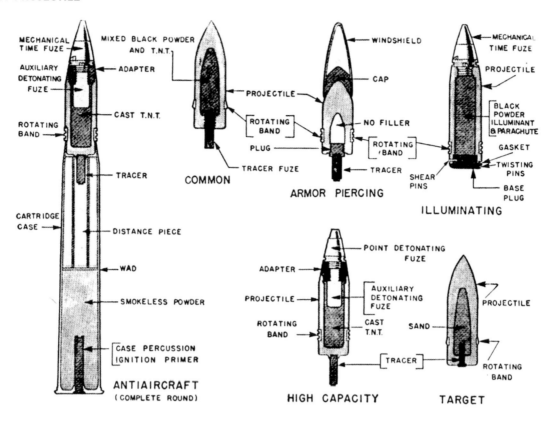

MECHANICAL TIME FUZE

AUXILIARY DETONATING FUZE

ROTATING BAND

CARTRIDGE CASE

MIXED BLACK POWDER AND T.N.T.

ADAPTER

CAST T.N.T.

TRACER

DISTANCE PIECE

WAD

SMOKELESS POWDER

CASE PERCUSSION IGNITION PRIMER

ANTIAIRCRAFT
(COMPLETE ROUND)

PROJECTILE

ROTATING BAND

PLUG

TRACER FUZE

COMMON

WINDSHIELD

CAP

NO FILLER

ROTATING BAND

TRACER

SHEAR PINS

ARMOR PIERCING

MECHANICAL TIME FUZE

PROJECTILE

BLACK POWDER ILLUMINANT & PARACHUTE

GASKET

TWISTING PINS

BASE PLUG

ILLUMINATING

ADAPTER

PROJECTILE

ROTATING BAND

POINT DETONATING FUZE

AUXILIARY DETONATING FUZE

CAST T.N.T.

TRACER

HIGH CAPACITY

PROJECTILE

SAND

ROTATING BAND

TARGET

PRIMER TYPES

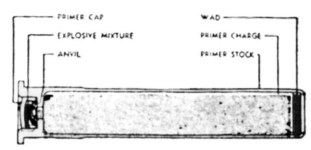

PRIMER CAP

EXPLOSIVE MIXTURE

ANVIL

WAD

PRIMER CHARGE

PRIMER STOCK

CASE PERCUSSION PRIMER, MARX X, MOD. 4.

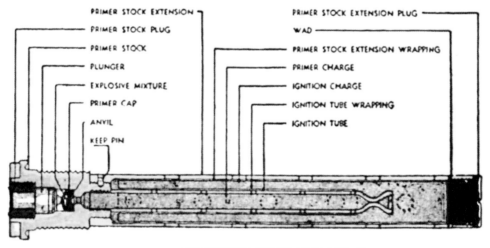

PRIMER STOCK EXTENSION

PRIMER STOCK PLUG

PRIMER STOCK

PLUNGER

EXPLOSIVE MIXTURE

PRIMER CAP

ANVIL

KEEP PIN

PRIMER STOCK EXTENSION PLUG

WAD

PRIMER STOCK EXTENSION WRAPPING

PRIMER CHARGE

IGNITION CHARGE

IGNITION TUBE WRAPPING

IGNITION TUBE

CASE PERCUSSION IGNITION PRIMER. MARX XTV.

The use of time-fused projectiles makes possible two general methods of control:

1. The *Barrage Method* in which the projectiles are set to burst in an area which is in the path of the target's flight and through which the target will pass. This is the simplest method because it permits the fuses to be set in advance and eliminates continual changes of the fuse settings.

2. The *Direct Method* in which the fuse of each projectile is set so that it will burst as close as possible to the target. This method is most effective for a given rate of fire because each projectile is meant to hit and do damage.

Magazines.—*Location.*—Powder is stowed in specially constructed rooms fully protected by armor if the ship has any, and as far as possible from the boiler and engine rooms. Magazines are placed near the guns they supply. Turrets have their powder magazines and shell storage space directly below them. All magazines are fitted with permanent connections for flooding quickly in an emergency. They are lighted with special water-tight lighting fixtures.

MAIN-BATTERY FIRE-CONTROL FUNDAMENTALS

There are three basic variables that must be determined with precision before a battleship's main-battery projectiles can be made to strike another ship or a target on land: (1) how much propellant to use for the projectile that is to be fired; (2) how to "lay," or aim, the gun (its elevation up and down and its train right and left); (3) the precise instant at which to fire the gun.

The first of these variables is the easiest to control. Generally, six 90-pound bags of smokeless powder would be employed. But in certain circumstances reduced charges would be used: for instance, against hardened targets on land in order to increase the projectile's angle of descent and strike the top of fortified positions, or to fall over and beyond a hill at enemy positions on a reverse slope.

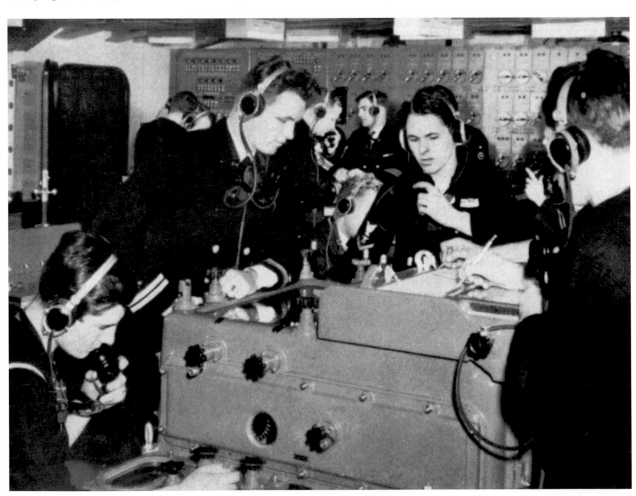

The main-battery plotting room on board *Alabama* during the war. (U.S. Navy)

The plotting room on board *Alabama*. Switches and breakers line the bulkheads, and rangekeepers are to the right (museum configuration). (Chris Bryant)

If the quantity of propellant is held constant, the two other calculations remain: how to lay the gun and how to time its firing. The most important data about aiming the main battery at targets came from one of the two main-battery fire-control directors. The ten fast battleships of the U.S. Navy in World War II all had two Mark 38 fire-control directors for their 16-inch guns: the forward one at the highest manned point of the ship, and the aft director just behind the stacks, at about half the height of the forward director (otherwise, it would not only have been above and behind the exhaust fumes coming out of the stacks but would also have impaired the ship's stability by adding more weight high above the waterline). An officer and many men were inside each tower to locate the target using either optical rangefinders or radar. They would determine the target's bearing, range, heading, and speed and transmit their data to the plotting room. There the numbers would be entered,

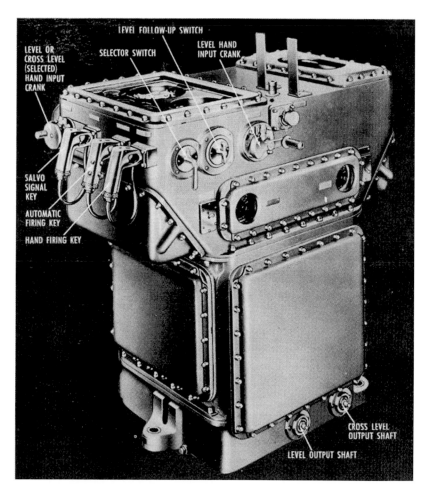

From a U.S. Navy training manual, the Mark 41 stable element (stable vertical), which corrected for the ship's pitch and roll. The main-battery guns were normally fired using pistol grips on the left end. (U.S. Navy)

either manually or automatically (electrically) into a computer known in the U.S. Navy as a "rangekeeper."

Alabama's computer was located in the plotting room, deep within the armored citadel of the ship. She used the Mark 8 rangekeeper, manufactured by Ford Instrument Company (not the automobile maker). The data was either transmitted into the computer by hand through knobs and dials after being received over voice circuits from the forward or aft fire-director towers, or transmitted electrically from instruments in the directors or from other instruments, such as the ship's gyro (for the firing ship's course), the ship's pitometer log (for the firing ship's speed), or the stable vertical (for the "level" and "cross-level" of the firing ship—that is, the extent to which it was pitching up or down or rolling left or right). Entering the data might take up to thirty seconds the first time, although subsequent recalculations to update the solution would usually be much faster. When the calculations were complete, electronic signals would be passed from the plotting room to the turrets to elevate the guns and rotate the entire turret so as to point the guns properly.

The guns would normally be fired from a trigger mechanism attached to the stable vertical, a few feet away from the rangekeeper in the plotting room. In relatively calm seas, the guns' train and elevation orders might be continuously corrected to allow for firing at virtually any moment. In more difficult seas, the guns might instead be set to move with the ship and could therefore only be fired when the system determined that the aim was correct.

ANTIAIRCRAFT DEFENSE IN THE *SOUTH DAKOTA*-CLASS BATTLESHIPS

The main role of the ten U.S. fast battleships rapidly evolved during 1943 into one of providing antiaircraft screening for the fast carriers. These carriers were appearing quickly in the U.S. Pacific Fleet beginning with USS *Essex* (CV-9), the lead ship of a new class of fleet carriers of which the Navy would have eighteen in commission before the end of the war. Other, smaller carriers, such as those of the light carrier *Independence*-class (CVL-22), were also assigned to the major carrier-led fast task forces of the war.

Since the carriers often dispatched their aircraft to attack enemy carriers or assigned their aircraft to support of ground operations, antiaircraft weapons on all other ships in the great task forces were critical. Antiaircraft fire might prove to be the last, or only, line of defense against air attack. The carriers and every other ship in the task forces were subject to dive- or glide-bombing attacks, torpedo-bomber runs, strafing, and, in the last ten months of the war, kamikaze attacks. In each of these scenarios, the attacking plane had to hold a steady course in order to aim its ordnance (or itself) at the target ship, giving antiaircraft units a good chance either to hit the plane or to rattle the pilot so that he could not stay on course and missed the target ship.

On the eve of World War II, U.S. Navy planners estimated an attacking bomber required 45 seconds to line up and bomb a target ship. This was, therefore, the amount of time available to antiaircraft units on ships like the *South Dakota*s to find a fire-control solution (i.e., predict where the plane would be when the antiaircraft ordnance would reach it) and fire. To target an attacking plane at 15,000 feet, it took 20 seconds to load and fire a gun and for the projectile to reach that altitude. The most difficult antiaircraft target of all was the dive-bomber, since it could plunge, at a speed of 300 knots, from 12,000 feet to the altitude at which it released its bomb in only 20 seconds.

For most of the war, the *South Dakota*–class carried three types of antiaircraft guns:

- *Twenty 5-inch/38-caliber guns* housed in ten dual mounts, five on each side of the ship on levels 01 and 02 of the superstructure (except for *South Dakota* herself, which had only four dual mounts on each side, dedicating the space saved to support an admiral and his staff, if *South Dakota* was serving as a flagship). These guns were controlled by a central fire director in one of four control towers, with input from the plotting room below deck. The 5-inch/38 guns were dual purpose, designed for use against both air and surface targets.

- Varying numbers of quadruple-mounted *Bofors 40-mm automatic cannons*. *Alabama* ultimately carried twelve mounts by the time of the Japanese surrender: two on the fantail on either side, one each on the top of main battery Turrets 2 and 3; two on each side of the main deck near the rear of the superstructure; two on level 02 of the superstructure just behind Turret 3; two on platforms on level 05 just behind the conning tower on the forward portion of the superstructure; and two on level 01 just forward of the forward most 5-inch gun mount on each side. These guns were controlled by directors located nearby and usually above the quadruple mounts, although they could also be aimed and fired locally if necessary.

- Varying numbers of *20-mm Oerlikon automatic cannons*. On board *Alabama*, these guns were located at each extreme of the ship, with six on the forecastle, six on the quarterdeck just behind Turret 3, and others scattered about the main deck and various levels of the superstructure, for a total of 52 by war's end. The 20-mm autocannons were aimed and fired by a sailor or Marine at each gun, with the assistance of several crewmen.

By the end of the war, *Alabama*'s antiaircraft fire was officially credited with downing 22 Japanese planes in combat.

Five-inch/38-caliber Guns

These dual-purpose guns were developed as a class between the wars when it became apparent that the increasing speed and altitude of attacking aircraft meant more powerful yet still agile guns were needed. While the main battery's 16-inch guns were the ship's most visibly imposing weapons, as the war progressed it was with their five-inch guns that *Alabama* and all the other fast battleships made their most notable contribution to the U.S. war effort in antiaircraft protection of naval formations based on aircraft carriers.

Alabama had ten 5-inch dual mounts for a total of 20 guns. On each side of the ship on the first superstructure level there were two mounts and on the second superstructure level, three mounts. In order from forward to aft, irrespective of the level on which they were located, the guns were numbered 1, 3, 5, 7, and 9 on the starboard side and 2, 4, 6, 8, and 10 on the port side.

The 5-inch guns were usually controlled by one of four Mark 37 directors known as Sky 1 (forward), Sky 2 (port), Sky 3 (starboard), and Sky 4 (aft). These were rotating towers located high above the main deck, containing optical and radar systems designed to determine the range, bearing, and rate of climb or descent of hostile aircraft. Any of the four directors could be given control over the laying and firing of any or all

A 5-inch/38-caliber mount on board *Alabama* (museum configuration). (Daniel Rogers)

Sky 1, the forward fire-control director for the 5-inch/38-caliber guns (museum configuration). (Daniel Rogers)

The upper handling room of a 5-inch/38-caliber mount (museum configuration). (Chris Bryant)

of the 5-inch mounts. They could track targets moving up to 400 knots horizontally or 250 knots vertically. The directors sent signals that, in conjunction with Mark 1A rangekeepers in the plotting room, rotated the 5-inch mounts and controlled the elevation of their guns via servo mechanisms. The guns could be elevated to a maximum angle of 85 degrees.

The 5-inch/38 guns used brass shell cartridges that weighed about thirty pounds when filled with powder. They did not use bag propellant as the main battery did, because as antiaircraft weapons they would often be firing rapidly at extreme angles of elevation. Inserting bags into a vertical barrel would have been impractical. The five-inch guns could be fired semiautomatically (immediately upon being reloaded). They ejected their cartridges automatically upon recoiling after firing.

Each mount consisted of the gun house itself, below which was an upper handling room and a lower handling room. A magazine surrounding the lower handling room stored the projectiles and cartridges. Two men normally worked in the magazine, removing the cartridges from their airtight cannisters and passing them through circular scuttles into the lower handling room. At least six sailors were stationed in the lower handling room, in which the projectiles were stored. The propellant-containing cartridges and the projectiles were raised up one level via separate hoists to the upper handling room.

The upper handling room kept a supply of ammunition and cartridges ready for fire and was resupplied from

below when these were running low. During firing, the upper handling room would use hoists to send cartridges and projectiles up to the mounts. When the mount was under control of one of the fire directors, the projectile's timed fuse would be set automatically based on data from the fire-control director as the projectile rose to the gun house from the upper handling room. The fuse would detonate the projectile, if all went as calculated, in the vicinity of the attacking aircraft. Later in the war, the majority of fuses in five-inch antiaircraft fire did not require such setting, as they were Mark 32 "variably timed," or proximity, fuses containing a radar element to detonate their projectiles close to aircraft. The Navy's Bureau of Ordnance estimated that the Mark 32 fuses provided a four-to-one overall advantage over regular, timed fuses.

Once in the mounts, the cartridges and fused projectiles would be removed from the hoists by a powder man and projectile man for each of the two guns. The men would place the propellant cartridge and the projectile onto a tray that would be power-rammed into the breech. The breechblock would close, and the gun would be ready to fire. When operating at peak speed and efficiency, the guns could be fired fifteen times per minute.

Also in the mount were the mount captain, stationed in the center rear of the mount; two individual gun captains, one for each gun; two hot-case men wearing asbestos gloves to pick up and remove any cartridges that were not automatically expelled out through an opening in the back of the mount (firing at an angle of elevation greater than 40 degrees rendered the auto-ejection system inoperable); and four men whose job was to be ready in case local fire proved necessary (a sight setter, a fuse setter, a pointer, and a trainer). This made for a crew of 13 inside the gun house of each mount.

Bofors 40-mm Automatic Cannons

The 40-mm Bofors gun was one of the most widely used and successful antiaircraft guns in the war. It served throughout the world on land and at sea in single, double, or quadruple mounts for ground and sea forces of many Allied and Axis nations.

These guns were first designed and developed by the Swedish firm Bofors in the early 1930s. The United States licensed production of the guns in 1941 and began placing water-cooled versions on its ships to replace 1.1-inch and .50-caliber guns, which were believed inadequate for the realities of modern antiaircraft warfare. The Navy's mounts would be power-driven and controlled by the gun captain using a Mark 51 director. This director had two handlebars, allowing the gun captain to move the director and its Mark 14 gun sight to track the path of the target aircraft. The Mark 14 employed gyros to measure the vertical and lateral rates of change of the target and thus permit the gun captain to "lead" the target properly. If director control failed for any reason, a ring sight allowed the pointer and trainer seated at each gun to take over and make aiming decisions. Normally, however, by squeezing a trigger mounted on the right handlebar, the gun captain at the director would fire.

The crew at each quadruple mount consisted of 11 men: the gun captain, the trainer, the pointer, four ammunition loaders, and four ammunition passers. The rounds were inserted by the loaders manually in clips of four into openings at the top of each gun. Thus the guns could only fire as fast as the loaders and passers could bring ammunition to them. After firing, the empty cartridges were ejected out the breech of each gun and through curved chutes down onto the deck of the gun mount in front of the guns.

The 40-mm high-explosive rounds were capable of reaching targets out to a range of over 11,000 yards. Because they were not time fused or proximity fused as the 5-inch rounds were, they had to impact the target aircraft before exploding, although often rounds were set to explode after covering much shorter distances in order to avoid hitting friendly ships or aircraft beyond a missed target aircraft.

Oerlikon 20-mm Automatic Cannons

Alabama's 20-mm guns were also based on a design licensed abroad, this time from the Swiss firm Oerlikon. They were free-swinging guns moved by the force applied

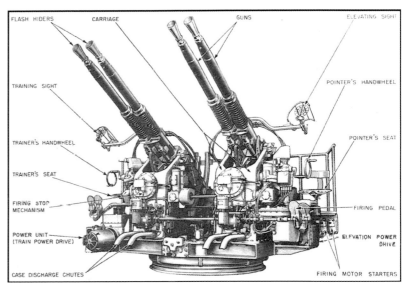

Quad 40-mm mount (U.S. Navy)

40-mm quad mount on *Alabama*'s starboard side. (Chris Bryant)

20-mm gun positions on the starboard side. (Chris Bryant)

by their crews. They were air-cooled, unlike the water-cooled 40-mm guns, and so could be located almost anywhere on the ship where space was available and the need was foreseen. They were the ship's last line of defense against attacking aircraft. Hearing them fire told crew members that danger was close.

Ammunition was supplied in drum magazines containing 60 rounds. The projectiles were usually contact-fused high-explosive shells, each weighing approximately half a pound (including its cartridge). The guns could fire up to 450 rounds per minute at targets up to 4,800 yards away and 10,000 feet in altitude. But since the drums contained only 60 rounds, the theoretical maximum rate of fire could not be sustained for long.

Provided the crew member manning the gun could squat low enough, the guns were capable of firing straight up, at an angle of 90 degrees. Each gun was protected by a thin splinter shield. Most on board *Alabama* were equipped with ring sights only, requiring the operator to rely on instinct to gauge the ship's own motion and lead the attacking aircraft appropriately; as the war drew to a close, some were given the same Mark 14 gyro-assisted sights used on the 40-mm's Mark 51 director. Each gun crew consisted of the gunner, a trunnion operator (to assist in raising and lowering the gun to the best height for the gunner), and two loaders.

In the middle part of the war, the 20-mm guns were at least as effective as the other two types in claiming kills of enemy aircraft. But with the dawn of the

20-mm Oerlikon gun (U.S. Navy)

BARREL

SPRING CASE

MAGAZINE

BARREL SPRING

SIGHT

SHOULDER REST

BREECH BAR

BREECH CASING

kamikaze era, an aircraft had to be nearly destroyed to eliminate the chance it could be steered into a ship, and the 20-mm gun's stopping power was regarded as insufficient.

COMBAT INFORMATION CENTER

Historian and submariner Timothy S. Wolters has termed the Combat Information Center (CIC) on board World War II U.S. Navy vessels "the brain of the warship." In the era of radar, the amount of data streaming to the commanding officer in combat situations was overwhelming. He could not possibly acquire information about surface, subsurface, or aerial contacts, evaluate it, keep track of it, and act on it all at once. Help came in

The Combat Information Center (museum configuration). (Chris Bryant)

the establishment of the Combat Information Center. Officers and men of the CIC would use the surface- and air-search radar screens along with the reports of lookouts and nearby ships and inputs from other sources to create a real-time plot of the seas and skies around the ship and give the commanding officer, gunnery officer, and other key stations accurate, relevant, and important information to enable good decisions and precise targeting.

The CIC on board *Alabama* was located on the third deck within the armored citadel. Officers and men of the ship's I Division became experts with the search radars. They used them to deadly effect during the Battle of the Philippine Sea, when they were the first to spot formations of Japanese planes over 140 miles away using the ship's SK radar. In conditions of poor visibility, CIC might effectively conn the ship, by virtue of providing the only navigation advice possible. For instance, during the typhoon of June 1945, as CIC officer Lieutenant Edward Wayne Bundy of Ogden, Utah, later recalled, CIC successfully guided the ship with its search radar when it passed between the separated but still floating bow of the cruiser USS *Pittsburgh* and the light carrier USS *Independence*, then battling a fire on her hangar deck.

AVIATION ON BOARD USS *ALABAMA*

U.S. Navy battleships and cruisers had been equipped with scout or spotter float planes since the 1930s. Launched from catapults, the planes searched for enemy vessels (including submarines), spotted naval gunfire (reporting to the firing ship where the shots were hitting relative to the target), towed target sleeves for crew antiaircraft practice, simulated torpedo-plane attacks to provide a realistic challenge during evasive-tactics training, and rescued downed aviators.

The first scout aircraft were biplanes, but by the time USS *Alabama* was being outfitted with her aircraft in 1942, the monoplane Vought OS2U Kingfisher was the standard scout plane for the battleships and cruisers of the U.S. fleet. *Alabama* carried three Kingfishers as she began her initial sea trials in 1942. When not aloft, two Kingfishers would be stowed on catapults, the third lashed to the deck between the catapults.

In order to take to the skies, the Kingfishers would be vaulted at full throttle by an explosive charge from one of two catapults on either side of the ship's fantail to the required takeoff speed of 60 knots. The catapults were on top of a turntable and could be pointed out to sea and into the wind.

The Kingfisher carried two .30-caliber machine guns (one forward that fired through the propeller, and one for the rear-seat radioman/gunner). It could also deliver 650 pounds of bombs (on any submarines spotted). But its main role on board *Alabama* was the more traditional one as the distant eyes of the ship in combat. Its low maximum cruise speed of 164 mph rendered it all but

A Vought OS2U Kingfisher approached the sled being towed by its ship. (NARA)

A Kingfisher scout plane is catapulted off the port side during World War II. (U.S. Navy)

Two of the Kingfisher floatplanes during the shakedown period. (U.S. Navy)

UNITED STATES NAVAL INSTITUTE

useless in air-to-air combat and was a major factor in the Kingfishers' replacement by war's end with the Curtiss SC Seahawk, which had a maximum speed of 313 mph.

Retrieving the scout planes was an intricate process. The battleship would first turn into the wind, to create a broad wake for the plane to land upon. This fresh patch of smoothed sea would ensure a much calmer landing than one made through waves. The battleship would tow a rope "sled," and the scout plane, after landing, would taxi onto it. A hook on the bottom of the plane's float caught a rope on the sled, and then the plane could be pulled closer to the battleship. As crewmen on board the battleship stood ready with long poles to keep the plane from striking the side of the ship, the crew of the scout plane would attach a hook lowered from the crane on the fantail to the plane. Then they, and their plane, would be hoisted aboard and placed either on the deck or back onto one of the catapults.

Although the aviators had some of the most exciting duties on board, the opportunities to take to the skies were actually infrequent. During the long periods when there were no bombardments or fleet actions requiring spotting or searching, the three crews remained on board ship. In 1944, Alabama's planes were launched 54 times spread out over three crews, meaning each crew flew on average only about once every three weeks.

PROPULSION

The South Dakota–class battleships presented their designers with a dilemma. They were to be more heavily armored than their immediate predecessors, the two battleships of the North Carolina–class. Yet they were required to be capable of approximately the same top speed, 27–28 knots. Moreover, these changes also had to be made without increasing the displacement of the vessels above the 35,000-ton limit of the naval arms-reduction treaties.

The only way to keep the displacement the same while increasing the armor protection was to save weight by shortening overall length. The four South Dakotas would be 680 feet long overall, as compared with the 728 feet 9 inches of the North Carolinas. Since the ships had the same beam, about 108 feet (so as to wedge into the Panama Canal's 110-foot-wide locks), the shorter length put the South Dakota at a serious speed disadvantage. As a simple matter of hydrodynamics, and with all other factors being

held constant, a longer vessel can move faster than a shorter one of the same width. Thus, to match the North Carolinas in speed the South Dakotas would have to be more efficient.

This was accomplished: the boilers and turbines of the South Dakotas' propulsion plant produced more power in considerably less space, at the cost of creating a ship that was cramped compared with the predecessor class. The distance from the front of North Carolina's Turret 1 to the rear of its Turret 3, roughly the length of the armored citadel, was 415 feet. On board Alabama, the same line ran about 370 feet.

The ship's eight boilers, constructed by Foster Wheeler, were of a type first successfully installed on the destroyer USS Somers (DD-381) in the mid-1930s. They created a pressure of 600 pounds per square inch, at which the steam could be "superheated" to 850 degrees Fahrenheit. The extra energy transferred to the steam when it was superheated was thus available to spin the turbines faster, but this temperature was the upper limit of what the boilers' water-carrying pipes could safely handle. Refinements in the turbine nozzles, steam piping, and other systems made possible the speed required to match North Carolina. The maximum (overload) shaft horsepower delivered by the four turbines on board the South Dakotas was 135,000, an increase from the 121,000 of the North Carolinas. The increase brought the maximum speed of the South Dakotas very close to the 28 knots of their predecessors.

The fuel bunkers of the South Dakotas, over 400 in all, were placed along the sides and bottom of the ship. Combined, they could hold over 2 million gallons of fuel oil. The fuel oil was loaded into them through ports located along a catwalk on the sides of the ship below the weather deck. While the quantity of oil they could store gave the South Dakotas a theoretical range of 17,000 nautical miles steaming at 15 knots, in practice Alabama was used as a floating gas station for the many destroyers and other vessels with smaller fuel capacities that always accompanied her. In 1945, Alabama reported that every three to five days she refueled four to six destroyers and she had to take on fuel herself from an oiler every four days.

In the boiler the fuel was ignited, and the energy produced transformed liquid water into steam. The water came from the sea. Since any salt or other seaborne impurities could rapidly damage the boilers and turbines, the seawater had to be exactly treated so that only pure water was introduced into the boilers. Evaporators located forward of the engine rooms treated 80,000 gallons of water per day, not only for use in the boilers but also for drinking, cooking, and washing. The ship's tanks could hold over 118,000 gallons of treated water.

After the steam had been produced, it was carried by piping into four groups of Westinghouse-built geared turbines. Each of the turbines had two sets of blades, oriented so that opening valves next to a given set of blades would turn the propeller shafts in the direction required to move the ship either forward or astern, as ordered by the conning officer.

Each of the four machinery spaces had a high-pressure and a low-pressure turbine. Steam first entered the high-pressure turbines and pushed through them, turning the turbines; the partially spent steam then flowed to the low-pressure turbine, which would consume most of the remaining energy. Since turbines have to work at very high speeds in order to be efficient (up to 6,000 rpm) but propellers must turn at much slower speeds, the output of the turbines was first

The shaft revolution indicator on board USS *Alabama* indicating the RPM range for one of the propeller shafts. (Daniel Rogers)

transmitted through reduction gears to decrease the rotational speed to one the propellers could safely handle, a maximum of about 180 rpm, but still at very high power. At the end of the process, a condenser collected the leftover steam, converted it to water, and fed it back to the boilers.

A pair of boilers was connected to each of the four sets of turbines. It was not necessary for all boilers to be operating at all times if the speed ordered by the conning officer did not require it. In port, often only one boiler at a time might be lit, in order to provide electricity.

The machinery space contained seven 440-volt AC electrical generators to provide current for the ship's lighting and equipment. They too had spinning turbines driven by boiler steam, but these were not connected to propeller shafts but instead drove electrical generators. Emergency diesel-powered generators were located directly fore and aft of the machinery spaces in case power from the main, steam-driven generators was disrupted.

Alabama began her service with four propellers, each of which had four blades. Over time, experiments with different configurations by the four ships of the *South Dakota*–class led by war's end to a reconfiguration of *Alabama*'s propellers for maximum speed and minimum vibration: four blades

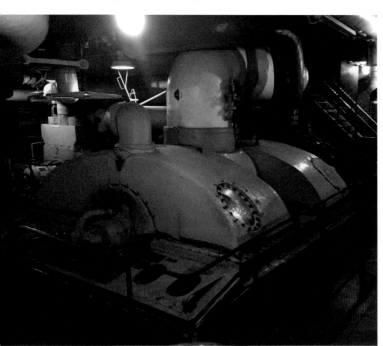

One of the low-pressure turbines on board *Alabama* (museum configuration). (Daniel Rogers)

on the two inboard propellers, five blades outboard. The inboard propellers were mounted on the end of long shafts that were supported by two struts extending downward from the hull. They were located just forward of the twin rudders. The outboard propellers were mounted at the end of skegs that ran along the outer edge on each side of the bottom of the hull.

Steering the ship was possible from one of four locations: the navigating bridge, the secondary conn high on the superstructure at level 08, the central station (emergency bridge within the armored citadel) on deck 3, and in each of the steering-engine rooms.

RADAR

In the mid-1930s, the world's leading military and technological powers began to develop a means of using radio waves to detect aircraft and vessels at great distances and calculate their range. The U.S. Navy called the system "radio detection and ranging," and the acronym *radar* soon came into general use.

A fireman at one of *Alabama*'s boilers. (U.S. Navy)

The propellers, rudders, skegs, and keel of *Alabama*'s sister ship USS *Indiana* (BB-58), with five-bladed propellers outboard attached to the skegs, and four-bladed propellers inboard at the end of exposed shafts. For most of her service, *Alabama* used this configuration. (NHHC)

Three radar-assisted fire directors, from left to right: the aft main-battery director, below and to the right, a Mark 57 director for the 40-mm guns below, and to the far right, Sky 4, the aft 5-inch/38 fire-control director (museum configuration). (Daniel Rogers)

Radar antennas on *Alabama* (museum configuration). (Daniel Rogers)

Radar would revolutionize the battleship. It made detection of both friendly and enemy forces possible in conditions of low or no visibility, facilitating night fighting. It meant that approaching enemy air forces could be detected over 100 miles out, albeit not consistently, giving the ships time to assume the most effective formation for antiaircraft fire. This warning also gave an opportunity for the precise vectoring of any accompanying friendly fighters toward the onrushing attackers. It allowed radarmen on board ship to see

representations of the impact of main-battery fire in the water near target ships and send corrections to those responsible for directing the fire and improving its accuracy—again, even at night.

The U.S. Navy was ready to begin installing radar units on board its ships in large numbers just as *Alabama* was being commissioned in 1942. Because radar technology was being continually developed by military, naval, and civilian researchers, the systems on *Alabama* would be upgraded throughout the war. These continual refinements gave the U.S. Navy a major advantage over all hostile navies.

There were two main types of radar systems on board *Alabama* and her sister ships: search radar and gunnery fire-control radar. When *Alabama* steamed from Norfolk on its first sea trials in November 1942, atop the foremast was the roughly square-shaped antenna for the sole type of search radar available at the time, known as SC. It had a maximum range of 50,000 yards. All fire-control directors, for the main and secondary batteries and the backup fire-control system in the conning tower, were equipped with radar antennas. The Mark 8 radar on both main-battery directors could track surface targets out to 40,000 yards and discern individual shell splashes up to 20,000 yards. The Mark 4 on the secondary batteries' directors could track planes out to 40,000 yards and larger ships to 30,000 yards. A Mark 3 radar unit was installed on top of the conning tower, along with a spotting glass and periscopes.

By the end of the war, *Alabama* had many updated radar systems, both for fire-control and search functions. The Mark 37 secondary-battery directors (Sky 1 through 4) had two radar antennas each: the Mark 12 to find the range and the Mark 22 for determining altitude. The Mark 12 could track at ranges up to 45,000 yards. The Mark 22, known for its antenna's distinctive shape as the "orange peel," was most useful for tracking extremely low-flying aircraft. The forward main-battery directors were now equipped with Mark 13 radar that could track surface targets out to 40,000 yards and identify individual shell splashes at roughly the same distance. The aft main-battery director continued to carry the Mark 8 installed earlier. In 1945, some of the 40-mm mounts were fitted with new Mark 57 directors, which included their own solid parabolic radar antennas. These directors enabled the mounts to fire without relying solely on the visual acuity and reflexes of their gun captains.

The superstructure of *Alabama* by 1945 bristled with new search-radar antennas. The most prominent was the rotating SK-2 radar with a parabolic antenna; it could detect aircraft out to over 150 miles. The SU, its antenna atop the foremast, was designed to counter the ability of the Japanese to intercept radar frequencies previously used, by operating at higher frequencies; however, it required greater power, which limited its usefulness. The SG and SR radar antennas were on the mainmast. The SG, with a small curved antenna, could detect a large target such as a battleship out to 45,000 yards and a bomber at low altitude at 30,000 yards. The SR system, with a large rectangular antenna, was designed primarily for aircraft detection and could spot planes at a theoretical maximum range of 200 miles.

The search-radar systems integrated an "Identification Friend or Foe" (IFF) component. Friendly planes and ships were equipped with transponders that would "squawk," or emit a signal, when interrogated by IFF. That signal would identify the aircraft or vessel as friendly. While it could not positively identify a contact as a foe, since transponders sometimes failed or malfunctioned, it could reduce the chances of friendly fire incidents. Most of the war's major powers employed such technology.

Countering enemy radar technology took on increasing urgency as the war progressed. In her major early-1945 refit, *Alabama* was equipped with electronic countermeasures that would confuse and jam enemy radar. Large radomes were attached amidships to the first superstructure level above the main deck on each side, and a smaller radome was placed at the top of the foremast. They were capable of broadcasting signals on all known Japanese frequencies.

Finally, radar was used in the Mark 32 VT, or proximity, fuses used on the 5-inch guns, in order to increase their lethality against Japanese aircraft. The VT fuses would detonate the shell when its radar component detected an object within the designated range.

INTERIOR COMMUNICATIONS

Four main systems provided internal wired communications:

- Critical parts of the ship had dial telephones that reached each other directly via an automatic switchboard.

- Loudspeakers provided general information to wide areas of the ship.

- Sound-powered telephones, which did not require electricity to operate, were worn by crew members who needed to be in constant communication with each other at critical moments, such as firing the main or secondary batteries.

- A second, auxiliary sound-powered system stood by in case it was needed.

Switches in the Internal Communications room on the fourth deck (museum configuration). (Daniel Rogers)

These systems were controlled by the Interior Communications Room on the starboard side of the fourth deck, within the armored citadel. It contained switchboards and generators for voice communication, alarms, signals, and steering circuits.

THE CONNING TOWER

In common with all U.S. battleships and cruisers constructed before or during World War II, *South Dakota*–class battleships had a thickly armored conning tower located at the front of the superstructure. During normal, noncombat operations, the commanding officer or another officer would *conn*, or direct, the course and speed of the ship from the navigating bridge, just in front of the conning tower. For much of its wartime life, *Alabama*'s navigating bridge was exposed to the elements, but it was enclosed during the ship's extensive refit at Puget Sound in early 1945.

Inside the conning tower, battleship commanding officers would be thoroughly protected while their ship was being targeted by enemy shellfire or aerial bombs. The armor plate around the conning position was 16 inches thick. Five slits in the forward wall of the armor provided limited visibility for those inside. To help overcome the disadvantages of directing the ship through slits, two periscopes were installed.

U.S. Navy commanding officers did not typically like having their visibility limited in that way and were reluctant to move inside the conning tower in combat situations. At the Naval Battle of Guadalcanal in November 1942, for instance, the commanding officer of *South Dakota* remained outside the conning tower, despite the peppering his superstructure received from Japanese medium-caliber guns. Luckily he escaped without wounds, but his actions proved an object lesson to the Navy on the limited usefulness of the heavily armored towers. During refits of older battleships of the World War I generation, the towers were often removed.

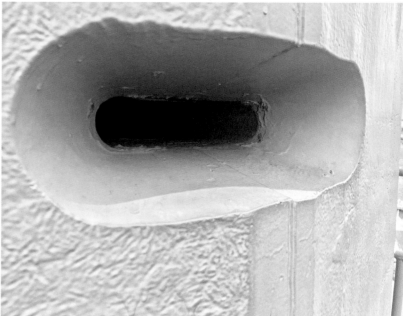

(left) The hatch to *Alabama*'s conning tower through its 16-inch armor (museum configuration). (Daniel Rogers)

(above) One of the five slits providing a view through the 16 inches of armor on the conning tower (museum configuration). (Daniel Rogers)

(bottom) The interior of the conning tower, including the helm (museum configuration). (Chris Bryant)

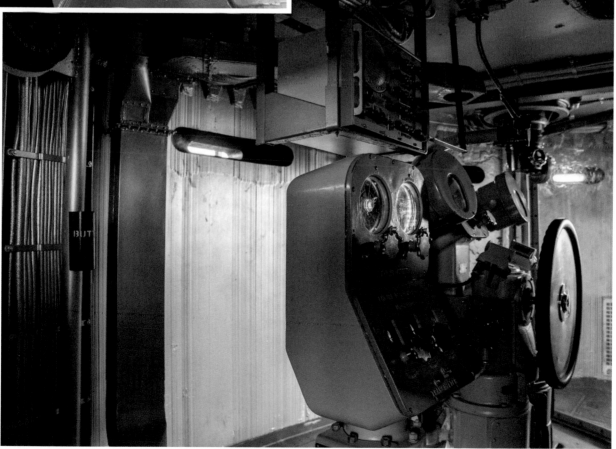

SISTER SHIPS

Alabama was the fourth and final of the *South Dakota* battleships to be commissioned in 1941 and 1942. The three other members also had distinguished combat records in World War II.

SOUTH DAKOTA (BB-57)

Nicknamed "Sodak," "Battleship X," "Big Bastard"

South Dakota was the most famous of her class during the war, primarily because her early commissioning meant she could participate in some of the desperate battles in the Solomon Islands in 1942. She was in action during the Battle of the Santa Cruz Islands on 26 October 1942, in which her crew claimed 26 aircraft shot down even as *South Dakota* was struck by two bombs.

It was, however, the night action of 14/15 November 1942, known as the Naval Battle of Guadalcanal, that proved to be *South Dakota's* sternest test of the war. Power failures in the middle of battle left her aft sections without electricity for 17 minutes, and her search radar was out for another 5. Her scout planes were set on fire by the muzzle blasts of her aft main battery and then blown overboard by subsequent concussions. *South Dakota* took 27 hits from Japanese shells ranging in caliber from 5 to 14 inches. She lost 38 crew members killed in action and a further 60 wounded. However, she never lost buoyancy or stability, and after an extensive period of repair, she would join *Alabama* as part of the British Home Fleet in 1943.

On 19 June 1944 at the Battle of the Philippine Sea, *South Dakota* was steaming near *Alabama* when she was hit by a 500-pound bomb dropped by a Japanese aircraft; 24 men were killed and 27 wounded. In a further tragedy near the end of the war, on 6 May 1945 at Okinawa, 3 men were killed immediately, 8 subsequently died, and 24 were injured when a canister of 16-inch high-capacity powder exploded as it was being passed into a magazine. (As an emergency damage-control measure, the magazines were flooded, and further damage was averted).

All in all, *South Dakota's* illustrious career included 64 enemy aircraft shot down.

Bombardment of Japan, 14 July 1945. USS *Indiana* (BB-58) fires a 16-inch salvo at Kamaishi, 250 miles north of Tokyo, and the site of the Imperial Japanese Iron Works. A second before, USS *South Dakota*, from which this photo was taken, fired the first salvo of the first gunfire bombardment of the Japanese home islands. (U.S. Naval Institute photo archive)

Like the other ships of her class, after being decommissioned in 1947 she remained in reserve until being stricken from the Naval Vessel Register on 1 June 1962. Some parts were sold to the state of South Dakota for use in a memorial in Sioux Falls, and others are on display in Willard Park of the National Museum of the United States Navy at the Washington Navy Yard in the District of Columbia. The remainder of the ship was sold for scrap.

South Dakota earned 13 battle stars in World War II.

INDIANA (BB-58)

Nicknamed "Hoosier Houseboat"

Indiana was commissioned in April 1942 and was first deployed in a combat setting at Guadalcanal later that year. Her role there was one of gunfire support for U.S. troops ashore in December 1942, taking the place of her badly damaged sister ship *South Dakota*. Her first Japanese aircraft kill came in November 1943, during Operation Galvanic in the Gilbert Islands.

During the U.S. invasion of the Marshall Islands on 1 February 1944, she was struck at night by *Washington* as she turned in front of that ship in complete darkness. Four men on board *Indiana* died as a result of the accident, and 200 feet of her armor plating were torn from her starboard quarter. Her only enemy-inflicted battle damage of the war was suffered during the Battle of the Philippine Sea on 19 June 1944 (the same day *South Dakota* was hit by a bomb). A crashing Japanese plane hit her starboard side on the waterline at frame 65. Debris flew onto the main deck, but there was neither serious damage nor any casualties.

Indiana participated in the Iwo Jima and Okinawa operations, emerging unscathed after shooting down three kamikazes near Okinawa. She was decommissioned in 1947, stricken from the Naval Vessel Register on 1 June 1962, and sold for scrap. Her mainmast, two gun mounts, and prow are on display outside Memorial Stadium on the campus of Indiana University in Bloomington.

Like *Alabama*, she earned nine battle stars in World War II.

MASSACHUSETTS (BB-59)

Nicknamed "Mighty Massy," "Big Mamie"

Commissioned in May 1942, USS *Massachusetts* was ready for the first U.S. operation against Nazi Germany and its allies and collaborators, the invasion of French Northwest Africa in November 1942 (Operation Torch). She was the flagship of the Western Naval Task Force. Since France had surrendered to Nazi Germany and pledged neutrality, its forces in Morocco and Algeria were compelled to resist the U.S. and British attack as an invasion of their territory. Thus *Massachusetts'* first and only main-battery fire against surface vessels would be directed at French ships. She was the first U.S. battleship to fire on an enemy battleship since the Spanish-American War.

On the morning of 8 November 1942, the battleship *Jean Bart*, confined to port in Casablanca, opened fire on *Massachusetts* with her 15-inch guns but missed. *Massachusetts* returned fire, striking *Jean Bart* seven times and ending the fire from the French battleship's main battery. Then *Massachusetts* fired on two French destroyers that had attacked her, sinking one of them. She also fired on coastal-defense batteries and detonated an ammunition dump. During these operations, she was struck between Turrets 1 and 2 by a 7.6-inch shell (fired from a shore battery) that penetrated the deck armor and by a 6.1-inch (155-mm) shell from the light cruiser *Primanguet*. There were no casualties.

Massachusetts engaged solely in Pacific Ocean operations for the remainder of the war. She participated in the Russell Islands and Gilbert Islands attacks of 1943, downing two aircraft in the latter. Like *Alabama*, she was a lucky ship for her crew, in that none were killed in combat throughout the war.

She was decommissioned in 1947 and stricken from the Naval Vessel Register on 1 June 1962. Again, like *Alabama*, *Massachusetts* was spared from the ship-breaking yard by the energetic advocacy of the citizens of her namesake state. On 12 June 1965, just months after *Alabama* was dedicated as a memorial, *Massachusetts* began her long life as a museum ship in Fall River, Massachusetts.

Massachusetts received 11 battle stars for her service in the Atlantic and Pacific.

(top) USS *South Dakota* (BB-57) during her shakedown period, July 1942. Note the four 5-inch mounts on each side, as opposed to the five mounts present on the other three ships of her class, including *Alabama*. (U.S. Navy)

(middle) USS *Indiana* (BB-58) at Majuro Atoll shortly after being struck in a collision with USS *Washington* (BB-56) (in the background) in the Marshall Islands, February 1944. (U.S. Navy)

(left) USS *Massachusetts* (BB-59) during the Naval Battle of Casablanca, 8 November 1942, during which she was struck by French shell fire. (NHHC)

THE CREW AND LIFE ON BOARD *ALABAMA*

THE WARTIME COMMANDING OFFICERS

The four men who would command *Alabama* during World War II were graduates of the U.S. Naval Academy between 1914 and 1919. All held the rank of captain while they were on board *Alabama*.

GEORGE BARRY WILSON
Born 27 March 1892–Died 4 December 1949

Commanding Officer, USS *Alabama*, 16 August 1942–17 March 1943

George Wilson brought a wide variety of experience at sea and ashore to his duty as the first commanding officer of USS *Alabama*. He was the only one of the wartime commanding officers to have had significant experience in naval aviation, although he was not an aviator himself.

Wilson was born in Norfolk, Virginia (like Captain Murphy after him—and USS *Alabama* herself). He attended the U.S. Naval Academy from 1910 to 1914 and had immediate sea duty on board USS *Delaware* (BB-28), seeing action against Mexico and then in the Atlantic during World War I. After the war, he was assigned to the Bureau of Aeronautics and to the first aircraft carrier of the U.S. Navy, USS *Langley* (CV-1). Subsequently he was assigned to battleships, such as USS *Utah* (BB-31) and USS *Mississippi* (BB-41), on the latter of which he served as gunnery officer. He was assigned to destroyer squadron staffs on two occasions, including from 1927 until 1930 in the Asiatic Fleet on board the destroyer tender USS *Black Hawk* (AD-9). Wilson ended the 1930s as executive officer of the light cruiser USS *Honolulu* (CL-48), from 1938 to 1940.

George Barry Wilson, first commanding officer of USS *Alabama*, during the shakedown period, January 1943. (NHHC)

Wilson served for extended periods in shore assignments between the wars, including several years at the Philadelphia Navy Yard, the Office of the Inspector of Naval Material, and at Pearl Harbor. He was in the Navy's personnel directorate (Bureau of Navigation) at the beginning of World War II.

Assigned to be the first commanding officer of *Alabama*, he took formal charge of that ship at her August 1942 commissioning. He led the ship through her sea trials ("shakedown") in the Chesapeake and the Atlantic.

Wilson fell seriously ill in March 1943 and had to be replaced suddenly as commanding officer of *Alabama* before she departed from Maine for her first operational cruise, in the North Atlantic around Canada, Iceland, and the United Kingdom. For three days after Wilson's departure, the ship's executive officer, Commander Neil Kittrell Dietrich, acted as the commanding officer.

After Wilson recovered, he was placed on the staff of Admiral Harold Stark, commander of U.S. Naval Forces Europe. Wilson retired in 1946 at the rank of rear admiral. In 1949 he died of a heart attack at Bethesda Naval Hospital at the age of 57 and was buried at Arlington National Cemetery.

FRED DURREL KIRTLAND
Born 6 November 1892–Died 6 October 1972

Commanding Officer, USS *Alabama*, 20 March 1943– 23 August 1944

Of the four wartime commanding officers of USS *Alabama*, Fred Kirtland was the only one with extensive shore and sea duty in engineering posts. Much of his career prior to arriving on board *Alabama* was devoted to studying the subject or leading engineering commands.

Kirtland was born in Salina, Kansas, and entered the U.S. Naval Academy from there in 1912. After graduation in 1916, his early assignments included USS *Wyoming* (BB-32) and postgraduate courses in engineering at Columbia University. Other engineering assignments in the 1920s and 1930s were at the fuel-oil testing plant at the Philadelphia Navy Yard, the Design

Captain Fred Kirtland (pictured above), relieved of command by Captain Vincent Murphy, departs on board one of the Kingfisher scout planes, 23 August 1944, Eniwetok Atoll. (U.S. Navy)

and Construction Division of the Navy Department, and the Navy Material Laboratory in New York City, where he was the officer-in-charge.

He did not go without significant sea duty during these first two decades. After *Wyoming*, his assignments included those as a lieutenant on board USS *California* (BB-44), engineering officer on board the new cruiser USS *Salt Lake City* (CA-25), executive officer of the repair ship USS *Medusa* (AR-1), and commanding officer of the destroyer USS *Breckinridge* (DD-148). He was assisting with the fitting out of the cruiser USS *Baltimore* (CA-68) in early 1943 when the sudden call to command *Alabama* was received.

Kirtland led *Alabama* as she first entered real wartime duties in the North Atlantic in the spring and summer of 1943. He took her back to Norfolk in August 1943, after which the ship transited the Panama Canal to spend the rest of the war in the Pacific. Kirtland was in command when *Alabama* earned her first five battle stars and oversaw her first main-battery bombardments at Kwajalein, Nauru, Ponape, and Saipan, as well as frequent antiaircraft fire, including during the Battle of the Philippine Sea.

He departed from *Alabama* in high style when relieved by Captain Murphy at Eniwetok in August 1944; he was catapulted as a passenger on one of the ship's Kingfisher scout planes over the lagoon and toward an assignment overseeing the Naval Ordnance Plant in Louisville, Kentucky. He returned to the Pacific in 1945 to command the Naval Operating Base at Okinawa and then held commands training the U.S. Atlantic Fleet and overseeing training for amphibious operations. He was placed on the retired list on 30 June 1951 at the rank of vice admiral. He died in 1972 in Roslyn, New York, at the age of 79 and was buried in nearby Flushing.

VINCENT RAPHAEL MURPHY SR.
Born 20 May 1896–Died 9 July 1974

Commanding Officer, USS *Alabama*, 23 August 1944–18 January 1945

Vincent Murphy had early and extensive command experience on board vessels of the U.S. Navy, more than any other of *Alabama*'s wartime commanding officers had before they took charge of the battleship.

Murphy was born in Norfolk, Virginia. He was a 1917 graduate of the U.S. Naval Academy and had his first sea duty on board the cruiser USS *Montana* (ACR-13, later renamed USS *Missoula* [CA-13]). But he was quickly shifted to duty in submarines, which gave him early opportunity for command. He served on the submarines USS *S-41*, USS *S-37*, and USS *S-11*. He commanded *S-37* as early as 1924 at the Asiatic Station and was later commander of *S-11*. His submarine duty ended in the mid-1930s, whereupon he spent several years on the staff of the U.S. Naval Academy. Thereafter he was navigator of the battleship USS *Texas* (BB-35) before beginning staff assignments with the Chief of Naval Operations and the Commander-in-Chief, Pacific Fleet (CINCPAC).

In this last assignment Murphy gained a degree of renown. He was serving at Pearl Harbor as the assistant war plans officer for CINCPAC, Admiral Husband Kimmel. As duty officer the weekend of 7 December 1941, he was on the phone with the admiral as they

Vincent Raphael Murphy Sr., third commanding officer of USS *Alabama*. (NARA)

both realized that Pearl Harbor was under attack. Murphy quickly sent out the famous message to all Pacific commands: "Air raid on Pearl Harbor. This is no drill."

Considered by Admiral James O. Richardson, Commander-in-Chief, U.S. fleet in 1940 and 1941, to be "the finest officer in the United States Navy," Murphy was transferred back to the mainland in the aftermath of Pearl Harbor. He spent two years at the Naval Postgraduate School before receiving command of *Alabama* in August 1944. Murphy commanded the ship as she screened carriers in the Western Caroline and Leyte operations and endured the typhoon of December 1944.

After being relieved as commander of *Alabama*, Murphy was assigned once more to the office of Chief of Naval Operations, where he served as the Navy's representative to the Munitions Assignment Board of the Combined Chiefs of Staff. He was then commander of the Office of Naval History from 1945 until 1946, when he retired from the Navy at the rank of vice admiral. He began a long second career as the executive vice president of the Navy Relief Society from 1946 to 1962. He died at Bethesda Naval Hospital in 1974 at the age of 79 and was buried at Arlington National Cemetery.

WILLIAM BERNARD GOGGINS
Born 10 September 1898–Died 27 December 1985

Commanding Officer, USS *Alabama*, 18 January 1945– 26 November 1945

William Goggins was the only commanding officer of USS *Alabama* who arrived with previous combat experience on board a U.S. Navy warship.

Goggins was born in Republic, Washington, and was nominated to attend the U.S. Naval Academy from Omak, Washington. He graduated in the class of 1919 and began his sea duty on the battleship USS *Idaho* (BB-42). He became an expert in radio communications and in the 1920s and 1930s served in several staff positions dealing with radio. This service brought him on board such battleships of the interwar era as *Arizona* (BB-39),

William Bernard Goggins, commanding officer of USS *Alabama*, 1944–1945, here shown before his service on board *Alabama*. (NARA)

Florida (BB-30), and *Pennsylvania* (BB-38). From 1929 to 1931, he served in the Radio Division of the Navy's Bureau of Engineering in Washington.

In the 1930s, Goggins' assignments became more varied and weighty. He was the executive officer of the destroyers USS *Hamilton* (DD-141) and USS *Noa* (DD-343), commanding officer of the destroyer USS *McCormick* (DD-223), and navigator on board the light cruiser USS *Trenton* (CL-11).

As World War II began for the United States, Goggins was executive officer of the light cruiser USS *Marblehead* (CL-12). During this assignment, *Marblehead* fought Japanese naval and air forces off the Dutch East Indies in February 1942. Goggins was severely burned by a bomb blast and evacuated from the ship. He narrowly escaped captivity by Japanese forces invading Java, thanks to the efforts of Navy physician Lieutenant Commander Corydon Wassell, who guided a group of wounded sailors from *Marblehead* to the south coast of Java for evacuation to Australia.

Goggins' most important assignment of all during the war, perhaps even eclipsing his later battleship command, called on his experience in radio. When he returned to Pearl Harbor in 1942, he was put in command of the Radio Intelligence Unit of the Intelligence Center for the Pacific Ocean Areas, the famed "Station HYPO" that earlier that year had correctly interpreted Japanese coded messages concerning their plans to attack Midway Island. Goggins remained in that post until being assigned as commanding officer of *Alabama* in January 1945.

On board *Alabama*, Goggins' leadership skill would be tested during antiaircraft operations near Okinawa, bombardments of Minami Daito Jima and Honshu, and the typhoon of June 1945. He was in command as *Alabama* returned to the United States at San Francisco on 15 October 1945. He was relieved by Captain Edward H. Pierce on 26 November 1945, whereupon he reported to the office of the Chief of Naval Operations and commanded the Naval Administrative Command of the Central Intelligence Group in Washington, a precursor of the CIA. He was chief of staff to the naval commandant of the Panama Canal Zone when

he retired in 1949. He was advanced to the rank of rear admiral at that time.

Goggins founded a computer and communications company, General Kinetics Institute, and lived in the Washington, DC, area until his death at age 87 in Fairfax, Virginia, as a result of an acute myocardial infarction. He is buried at Arlington National Cemetery.

CREW DIVISIONS ON BOARD USS *ALABAMA*

Each enlisted member of the crew was assigned to one of 27 divisions. Each division lived together and shared a head (washroom) and locker areas.

DIVISION	DUTIES OR STATION
1	Main Battery Turret 1, 16-inch/45 guns
2	Main Battery Turret 2, 16-inch/45 guns
3	Main Battery Turret 3, 16-inch/45 guns
4	U.S. Marine Detachment/20-mm antiaircraft guns
5	5-inch/38 guns, starboard side, Mounts 1, 3, and 5
6	5-inch/38 guns, port side, Mounts 2, 4, and 6
7	5-inch/38 guns, starboard side, Mounts 7 and 9
8	5-inch/38 guns, port side, Mounts 8 and 10
9	20- and 40-mm antiaircraft guns
10	20- and 40-mm antiaircraft guns
A	Engineering auxiliary
CR	Communications radio
CS	Communications signal

DIVISION	DUTIES OR STATION
CY	Communications yeomen
E	Engineering/electrical
EX	Master-at-Arms and cooks
FA	Fire control, antiaircraft
FM	Fire control, main battery
H	Medical, dental, and hospital corpsmen
I	Radar and Combat Information Center
L	Lookouts/band
N	Navigation/quartermasters
PA	Propulsion aft
PF	Propulsion forward
R	Repair and damage control
S	Supply, cooks, and bakers
V	Aviation
W	Wardroom steward's mates

U.S. MARINE CORPS DETACHMENT

From the first days of the U.S. Marine Corps in 1775, a primary duty of Marines was to serve on board U.S. naval vessels. They had to be ready to act as boarding parties against enemy ships, form police forces of a sort on board their own ships, and seize and establish bases ashore for the Navy as necessary.

On board *Alabama*, as on all battleships, cruisers, and aircraft carriers during World War II, there was a Marine Detachment. The numbers assigned varied between 66 and 100 Marines. They manned the brig, served as the color and honor guards for the ship, and formed the ship's Division 4, which manned 20-mm antiaircraft guns.

When not fulfilling these primary duties, the Marines were usually engaged in routine maintenance and cleaning activities. Marine William Robert Miller of Selma, Alabama, recalled reporting for duty on board *Alabama*, dry-docked at Pearl Harbor in January 1944, only to be assigned immediately to scrape barnacles from the bottom of the ship. A few Marines were always detailed as mess attendants, cooks, barbers, and bakers. Since the pride of the Marine Corps is each Marine's skill as a rifleman, they would occasionally hold practice on the ship, suspending targets above the ship's prow and firing from the top of main battery Turret 2, some 80 yards away.

At the end of the war, some of *Alabama*'s Marine Detachment were sent ashore to Japan to help demonstrate U.S. power and otherwise establish the first presence of the massive occupation force to come. The *Alabama* Marine Detachment, then commanded by First

Lieutenant Wade Porter Bettis of Boring, Oregon, was transferred to the attack transport USS *Garrard* (APA-84) on 19 August, just four days after Japan had accepted U.S. surrender terms. Ten days later, after Japanese-language instruction, practice in debarkation, and instruction about the assignment, Bettis led his men ashore.

The Marines were deployed to an industrial area and ordered to set up a perimeter and await further instructions. They remained ashore for only one week but were a vital, visible sign of the U.S. victory to the Japanese populace at the time of the surrender ceremonies in Tokyo Bay on 2 September. They neither encountered resistance nor learned of any. In their brief sojourn, they met English speakers eager to become friends and offer hospitality. As they returned aboard, they were sprayed and dusted to prevent any contagion among the Japanese populace from spreading to their shipmates. Their brief occupation duty brought to a close, they steamed with their ship first to Okinawa, then Hawaii, and finally San Francisco.

Alabama's Marine Detachment assembles on the forecastle. (U.S. Navy)

FOOD ON BOARD *ALABAMA*

The crew ate in four separate areas: one each for officers, warrant officers, chief petty officers, and the petty officers and junior enlisted men. The commanding officer had a separate formal "mess" (dining room), used on infrequent occasions.

While the quality of the food was generally far superior to what soldiers or Marines ashore consumed in combat conditions, there was still much about it that left men longing for home cooking.

Powdered milk and powdered eggs, reconstituted using fresh water from the evaporators, were an all-too-frequent staple, as were beans and chipped beef on toast (not-so-affectionately called "shit on a shingle" by the sailors). Bologna sandwiches or Army K-rations washed down with strong coffee were frequently served when the crew was at battle stations for prolonged periods. On rare occasions, such as holidays, there might be turkey. When the supply situation was good, pork chops, hamburgers, vegetables, and other foods that reminded them of home might be served.

The ship had a soda fountain / ice cream stand of the sort that sailors throughout the Navy called a "gedunk" (pronounced GHEE-dunk). Long lines would quickly develop when ice cream was available, and those at the end of the lines ran the great risk of waiting for hours to no avail, as the supply of ice cream was always exceeded by the demand.

(top) The commanding officer's formal dining room (museum configuration). (Chris Bryant)

(right) The "gedunk" ice cream fountain open for service during the war. (U.S. Navy)

(below) Chow line (U.S. Navy)

MEDICAL CARE

The H Division of *Alabama* comprised the physicians, dentists, and pharmacist's mates, ready to handle many routine cases of sickness and a variety of combat wounds for over 2,000 officers and men. Their facilities consisted of an operating room, examination room, bacteriological lab, sterilizing room, X-ray darkroom, isolation ward for quarantining those with communicable dis-

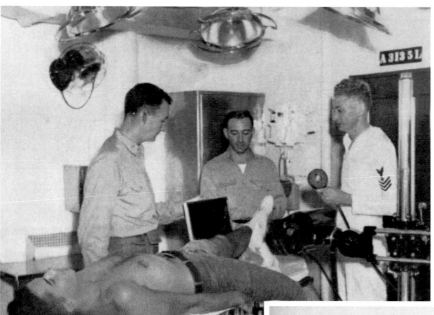

The sick bay in operation during the war. (U.S. Navy)

eases, and dispensary (pharmacy). The sick bay was air-conditioned and contained sufficient beds for numerous simultaneous casualties.

In combat scenarios, larger ships such as *Alabama* would often have the nearest medical facilities suitable for handling certain kinds of wounds. In some cases, their medical personnel might be needed on nearby ships that had been hit, most notably when the destroyer USS *Borie* (DD-704) was struck by a kamikaze in August 1945 (see "Battle Star 9," on page 93). In December 1943, the destroyer USS *Boyd* (DD-544) was hit by fire from a shore battery while attempting to rescue a downed U.S. aviator. Eleven men were killed instantly and eight wounded. The

three most serious cases were transferred directly to *Alabama*. One of those, with abdominal shrapnel wounds, subsequently died. Since *Alabama* was heading next into port at Espiritu Santo, his remains were not buried at sea but retained in one of the ship's refrigerated compartments.

The most serious casualties involving the crew of *Alabama* came during the Mount 5 accident of February 1944 (see "Mount 5 Accident" box on page 81). The medical staff could do nothing for five who died except prepare their remains for burial at sea. The staff treated the punctured lungs, serious burns, broken limbs, and other wounds of 11 others, all of whom survived. Seven of the wounded remained on board, and the other 4 were transferred to the hospital ship USS *Relief* (AH-1) when *Alabama* reached Majuro. After a month on board *Relief*, they were sent to Pearl Harbor and then the mainland United States.

A wounded sailor is transferred to *Alabama* for care from a destroyer. (U.S. Navy)

UNITED STATES NAVAL INSTITUTE

Alabama at Efate in the New Hebrides. (U.S. Navy)

CREW LIFE: SHORE LEAVE

Alabama's voyages afforded her crew only a few chances for shore leave in vibrant locales with abundant night life and social opportunities. Urban areas where the crew went ashore included Norfolk, Virginia; Portland, Maine; Reykjavík, Iceland; Pearl Harbor, Hawaii; Puget Sound, Washington; and Tokyo. In Norfolk, movies, burlesque shows, lounges, and other establishments catering to sailors' desires were available. The same was true of Pearl Harbor and Puget Sound. The visits to Reykjavík were far more restrained, as many sailors felt the local populace's sympathies in the war to be suspect and their attitude to the American sailors reserved.

Much more frequently, if less enjoyably, some of the crew were allowed to leave the ship for brief periods while she was at anchor off Pacific islands and atolls, such as the New Hebrides, Fiji, Eniwetok, Majuro, or Ulithi. These islands were not remembered fondly

When American League pitchers still batted: Bob Feller swings and connects in a baseball game while on shore leave in the Pacific. (U.S. Navy)

by many crew members. Radarman 2nd Class Peter Fernandez of Parkersburg, West Virginia, who kept a detailed diary of his life on board ship, referred to both Majuro and Ulithi as "hell holes." Groups of sailors were taken in whaleboats to shore, where they were usually given two warm beers apiece. Seaman 1st Class Earl Smith of Elyria, Ohio, recalled using compressed carbon dioxide to cool the beers.

Once ashore at such a remote spot, there was little to do other than swim, stand around, gamble (which was against regulations), or play baseball. Baseball games among the ship's own crew or against the crews of other anchored ships were a popular pastime. Of course, *Alabama* had an advantage over every other team she met on the diamond when Chief Petty Officer Bob Feller, future Hall of Fame fastball pitcher, was playing. Feller later recalled 10,000 spectators at some games in the New Hebrides, on Fiji, and on other coral islands, and playing "at 1 and 3 o'clock in the morning in Iceland while the sun was out."

Alabama sailors with their two beers on a Pacific beach. (U.S. Navy)

SAILORS OF COLOR ON BOARD *ALABAMA*

All branches of the U.S. armed services were segregated during World War II. The segregation regime in the Navy was especially harsh. As of June 1940, 18 months before the war, the Navy had only 4,007 Black sailors, all of whom were enlisted men. Only six of these sailors served in any capacity other than as steward's mates, the men who worked in the officers' wardroom and cleaned officers' billets. The Navy hierarchy resisted attempts to integrate ships, reasoning that White sailors would not submit themselves to discipline from Black superiors and that all-Black crews were impractical.

Since 1901, Filipinos had been permitted to enlist in the Navy. On board *Alabama* and every other ship in the Navy, they too were restricted to mess duty prior to the end of World War II.

All sailors, including the steward's mates, were required to have battle stations. Indeed, one of the earliest heroes of World War II was one such sailor, Doris Miller, who received the Navy Cross for his heroism on board USS *West Virginia* (BB-48) at Pearl Harbor, when he helped the wounded and manned a gun (for which he was not trained) after his assigned battle station was destroyed by a torpedo. Five Black sailors on board USS *Intrepid*

Alabama's W Division of steward's mates. (U.S. Navy)

(CV-11) were awarded the Navy Cross for their efforts in downing a kamikaze plane that subsequently crashed into their 20-mm gun tub during combat near the Philippines in October 1944.

On board *Alabama*, the steward's mates of W Division were, as their photograph in the ship's cruise book demonstrates, as segregated as those anywhere else in the Navy. They were the only division on the ship that was not issued "watch buttons" to indicate the division and watch to which the men were assigned. Yet they are remembered for more than serving as wardroom orderlies and cleaners of officers' quarters. Steward's Mate 2nd Class Blanchard Nelson "Speedy" Fleet of Ascension Parish, Louisiana, represented the entire ship in a boxing match against the crew of *Indiana*. Steward's Mate 1st Class Robert Lee Langston, born in the capital, Montgomery, of the state that gave his ship her name, was standing near Mount 5 during combat on 21 February 1944 when he was struck by metal fragments and killed (see "The Mount 5 Accident" box on page 81). He was buried at sea with the four killed inside the mount.

FROM POLLYWOGS INTO SHELLBACKS (AND BLUENOSES, AND GOLDEN DRAGONS)

For centuries, mariners have engaged in a rough initiation ritual when their ships crossed the equator. Those on board, officers and men alike, who have never crossed the line before, scorned as "Pollywogs" or "Slimy Pollywogs," are hazed as part of a two-day ritual by the "Shellbacks," who have been initiated on previous voyages.

Because of the often painful, embarrassing, and (temporarily) disfiguring treatment of the Pollywogs by the Shellbacks, the ritual was vividly remembered by all who underwent it on board *Alabama*. After finishing her initial deployment in the North Atlantic in August 1943, she returned for a brief supply and dry-docking visit to her birthplace at the Norfolk Navy Yard. She proceeded through the Panama Canal on her way, ultimately, to participate in Operation Galvanic in the Gilbert Islands in late November. On 2 September 1943, at approximately longitude 120 degrees west, *Alabama* was due to cross the equator. Shellbacks such as Musician 2nd Class Marvin Leo Melsha of Cedar Rapids, Iowa, who had served on board USS *Lexington* (CV-2) when she was sunk in the Battle of the Coral Sea in 1942, were entitled to initiate Pollywogs into the "Order of Neptune." "Subpoenas" signed by "Davy Jones" were issued to Pollywogs to appear before an elected "King Neptune," who, it threatened, would feed anyone failing to do so to the "Monsters of the Deep."

Chief Specialist Thomas Roy Bowers of Buffalo, New York, had enlisted in the Naval Reserve in December 1942 and reported aboard *Alabama* at Placentia Bay in May 1943. The ship's next crossing of the equator would be his first. In a journal he kept during the war, he recalled being made to stand atop Turret 1 the night before the equator crossing wearing skinny pants, a life jacket, baseball shin guards, and a catcher's mask and shouting at five-minute intervals, "I am the Father of Pop Fly!" He and many others were told to be on the lookout for "Davy Jones," and when he arrived, they paraded around the ship, to the mirth of the Shellbacks.

At 0800 on 2 September, the real initiation began. Bowers saw seven chief petty officers on top of Turret 3 being instructed to sing the folk song "Home on the Range." All the Pollywogs received "haircuts," which were usually nothing more than random gouges of their heads or perhaps intricate designs, either of which would require the new Shellback to completely cut off his hair in order to even it out. Shellback Radarman 2nd Class Harry Randolph Peaper of Capitol Heights, Maryland, recalled gleefully smearing grease into the Pollywogs' remaining hair and then dousing them with water from a hose. Many were beaten with large paddles in front of "King Neptune," and a large pool was constructed aft of Turret 3 in which Pollywogs were dunked. Few seemed to mind the process once it was over, and they looked forward to being Shellbacks at a future ceremony.

Alabama was a rare ship in the U.S. Navy in World War II in that three significant geographical lines

Proclamation of Membership in the Royal Order of Bluenoses for *Alabama*'s executive officer, Commander Neil K. Dietrich, 7 June 1943. (NHHC)

were crossed, all more than once in each direction: the Arctic Circle on 7 June 1943, the equator on 2 September 1943, and the International Date Line on 12 September 1943, just days after the hazing in front of "King Neptune." The crossing of the Arctic Circle entitled the sailors to membership in the "Royal Order of the Bluenose," and the crossing of the International Date Line to join the "Imperial Domain of the Golden Dragon." Neither of these line crossings, though, were accompanied by the sort of festivities associated with the appearance of "King Neptune" at the equator.

Shellback initiation ceremonies, 2 September 1943. (U.S. Navy)

HALL OF FAME BASEBALL PITCHER BOB FELLER REMEMBERS HIS SERVICE ON BOARD *ALABAMA*

"I'm Still a Navy Man at Heart," *Proceedings*, June 2008

BOB FELLER (1918–2010), THE LEGENDARY PITCHER FOR THE CLEVELAND INDIANS, INTERRUPTED A STUNNING CAREER IN THE MAJOR LEAGUES TO ENLIST IN THE NAVY AT THE START OF WORLD WAR II. AS CHIEF PETTY OFFICER ROBERT FELLER, HE PARTICIPATED IN SOME OF THE BEST-KNOWN SEA BATTLES IN THE PACIFIC. WHEN THE WAR WAS OVER, HE RETURNED TO THE MOUND AND RESUMED A STRAIGHT "SHOT TO STATION"—THE BASEBALL HALL OF FAME. HERE'S HIS ACCOUNT OF HIS MILITARY SERVICE AND WHAT IT MEANT TO HIM.

I never have to strain my memory to recall the day I decided to join the Navy. It was 7 December 1941. I was driving from my home in Van Meter, Iowa, to Chicago to discuss my next contract with the Cleveland Indians, and I heard over the car radio that the Japanese had just bombed Pearl Harbor. I was angry as hell.

I'd spent almost six full seasons in the major leagues by then, with a record of 107 victories and 54 losses, and I had a family-related draft exemption, but I knew right then that I had to answer the call. I arrived in Chicago late that afternoon to meet Cy Slapnicka, the Indians' general manager, who had come there to talk about my contract for 1942, and told him about my decision. I then phoned Gene Tunney, the former world heavyweight boxing champion and an old friend. A commander, Gene was in charge of the Navy's physical training program. He flew out from Washington and swore me in on Tuesday, 9 December.

After my basic training, the Navy made me a chief petty officer and assigned me as a physical training instructor. It was valuable in its way, but I wanted to go into combat. I'd had a lot of experience with guns as a kid, so I applied for gunnery school and sea duty. After four months of naval gunnery school in Newport, Rhode Island, I was assigned to a battleship, the USS *Alabama* (BB-60), as a gun captain on a 40-mm antiaircraft mount that had a crew of 24.

Action in the North Atlantic—and the Pacific

I got what I wanted. The *Alabama* spent six months escorting convoys in the North Atlantic, and then—in August 1943—went through the Panama Canal and headed for the Central Pacific. Over the next two years, we saw action off Tarawa, and in the Marshalls, the Carolines, and the Philippines. We bombarded beaches to support amphibious assaults, served as escorts for aircraft carriers, and fended off kamikaze attacks. . . . We survived a typhoon that pummeled us with 80-knot gusts off the Philippine coast. The *Alabama* never lost a man to enemy action. The people we had on the gun crews were very good shots.

In March 1945, I was sent to Great Lakes Naval Training Center and managed the baseball team there. In the third week of August, just 15 days after the United States dropped the atomic bomb on Hiroshima, I went on inactive duty. It was back to baseball after that. I rejoined the Indians on 23 August and pitched eight games. I won five and lost three.

Serving in the military is almost always a defining moment for any young man or woman. You're young and impressionable. You meet a lot of new people, and you travel to new places. You learn to be on time, how to follow, and, eventually, how to lead.

You Never Forget Combat

But it makes a difference when you go through a war, no matter which branch of the service you're in. Combat is an experience that you never forget. A war teaches you that baseball is only a game, after all—a minor thing, compared to the sovereignty and security of the United States. I once told a newspaper reporter that the bombing attack we lived through on the *Alabama* had been the most exciting 13 hours of my life. After that, I said, the pinstriped perils of Yankee Stadium seemed trivial. That's still true today.

You and your comrades never lose touch. I've gone to my share of *Alabama* reunions, and all of us treat each other as shipmates no matter what else we've done or accomplished—or haven't—over the years. I still remember with pain the sailor who stopped by my compartment to talk baseball during one of our North Atlantic convoy runs. A few minutes later, he was missing. Apparently he'd fallen overboard into rough seas—an accident of war.

Like anyone who has been under fire, I'm certainly not a war-booster. But I still believe, as I did that grim

Chief Specialist Robert Feller, Hall of Fame pitcher for the Cleveland Indians, at his 40-mm gun mount on board USS *Alabama*, late 1942 or early 1943. (U.S. Navy)

Sunday afternoon in December 1941, in a strong and well-equipped military and in the values that being in the service instills in the young men and women who don the uniform. I'm well aware of the hardships that our servicemembers are enduring right now.

Serving Your Country

For myself, I wouldn't be unhappy if they re-imposed a draft—not just because we need more troops to meet our needs, but because going through military training is such a character-builder for young people. Everyone ought to serve his or her country for a couple of years or more, even in times of peace.

I was at Great Lakes Naval Training Center a few months ago, where I'd been invited to speak to the graduates of the Navy's basic school, and someone asked whether I'd urge my grandson to sign up, as I had done. My answer was a resounding yes.

I'm still a Navy man at heart. And I'm proud to have served.

TYPHOONS

The Japanese word *kamikaze* means "divine wind" and is a reference to two typhoons in the 13th century that sank Mongolian invasion fleets. It is a bitter coincidence that, just as *Alabama* and the other ships of the Pacific Fleet were facing attacks from kamikaze aircraft, they would encounter two actual typhoons of immense power.

In December 1944, *Alabama* was one of eight battleships, seven fleet and six light aircraft carriers, 15 cruisers, and approximately 50 destroyers that were operating between 250 and 300 miles east of southern Luzon, in the Philippine Sea. They had been moved to this area by the Third Fleet's commander, Admiral William Halsey, so as to be able to refuel farther away from Japanese air bases on Luzon.

Meteorology at the time was primitive compared to that of the 21st century. Without satellites or the consistent and widespread application of radar to weather forecasting, commanding officers had to rely on radioed reports of data from weather observers to recognize the presence of tropical cyclones ahead in time for ships to avoid them.

Halsey's meteorologists did not get good data and thus failed to make timely and accurate recommendations. The fleet commander unknowingly sent many ships into what proved to be the heart of an approaching typhoon with 60-foot waves and winds estimated at over 145 mph. Destroyers were especially vulnerable, because of their smaller size and need for frequent refueling. Those that were not refueled in time lost the ability to maneuver directly into the waves and were at particular risk of capsizing. Three destroyers did capsize and sink, and nearly 800 sailors were reported lost from the typhoon. Three aircraft carriers experienced fires as planes broke loose and struck other planes or the ships' structure. A total of 146 planes were lost due to fires or other damage or by being washed overboard.

This typhoon, now known as Typhoon Cobra (but bitterly nicknamed "Halsey's Typhoon" by some in the Navy at the time), was to be one of the most vivid memories for *Alabama*'s crew. Seaman 1st Class Joel Monroe Holmes of Dalton, Georgia, remembered watching, at one moment, ships ahead looming above his own ship on the crest of a giant wave and in the next seeing them far below as *Alabama* rose on the same wave. He saw *Alabama*'s forecastle go 25 feet

under the water. Machinist's Mate 3rd Class John Matwey of Wilmington, Delaware, a member of the ship's antiaircraft-fire-control FA Division, was on a platform at the top of the ship. He spotted a sailor who had been washed overboard from another ship bobbing alone among the towering waves. At one point he noted on the stable element at his position that the ship had rolled 24 degrees; he had been told

Admiral William F. Halsey at the time of the December 1944 typhoon. (NARA)

previously that the danger point was 22-1/2 degrees. The ship's war diary reported rolls of 25 to 30 degrees. The captain's boat was knocked loose from the deck rings holding it down and washed overboard. Ammunition boxes welded to the forecastle deck were ripped loose. Both the scout planes on board were so badly damaged as to be declared total losses.

All the while, life on board ship continued. Sailors had to hold on to their seats with one hand and eat with the other. They locked their legs around their stools and dealt with food trays that slid back and forth on the table.

Almost six months later, in June 1945, a second typhoon ("Connie") struck the Third Fleet under Halsey's command. *Alabama* was about 600 miles

The waves of "Halsey's Typhoon" as viewed from escort carrier USS *Kwajalein* (CVE-98). (NHHC)

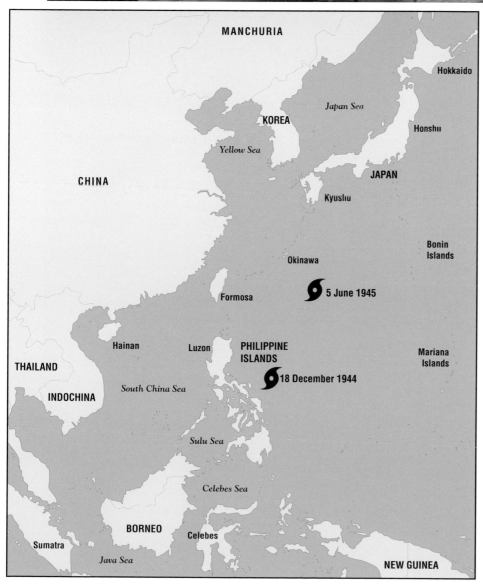

MANCHURIA

Hokkaido

Japan Sea

KOREA

Honshu

Yellow Sea

CHINA

JAPAN

Kyushu

Bonin
Islands

Okinawa

🌀 5 June 1945

Formosa

Hainan

Luzon

PHILIPPINE
ISLANDS

Mariana
Islands

THAILAND

🌀 18 December 1944

South China Sea

INDOCHINA

Sulu Sea

Celebes Sea

BORNEO

Celebes

Sumatra

Java Sea

NEW GUINEA

Locations where the *Alabama* was caught by the typhoons of 1944 and 1945. (Kelly Oaks)

northeast of her position during the first typhoon. The Third Fleet fared much better this time, but still six lives were lost. At 115 mph, the typhoon's winds were significantly less powerful but severe all the same. No ships were lost, but the bow of the cruiser USS *Pittsburgh* broke off. In this storm, a total of 76 aircraft were destroyed after breaking loose.

The Pacific Fleet responded to the typhoons by setting up new weather stations in the Caroline Islands, the Philippines, Iwo Jima, and Okinawa, as well as offices to coordinate the meteorological data on Leyte and Guam.

ADMIRAL RICHARD BYRD'S MORALE-BOOSTING VISIT

On 16 July 1945, renowned polar explorer Rear Admiral Richard Evelyn Byrd Jr. came aboard *Alabama* when she was 350 miles east of the Japanese home island of Honshu. Byrd was a household name in the United States and a legend in the U.S. Navy. A 1912 graduate of the U.S. Naval Academy, he had been one of the earliest naval aviators. Acting as navigator in a two-man crew, he flew on what the United States claimed as the first flight over the North Pole in 1926. Again serving as navigator, Byrd was one of four men in the first flight over the South Pole in 1929. He made numerous other Antarctic journeys; in one he spent five months by himself in a weather station in the winter of 1934, suffering from frostbite and nearly dying of carbon monoxide poisoning.

Thus when he came aboard *Alabama* via the bosun's chair as she was about to bombard Hitachi (see "Battle Star 9" on page 93), the crew would find he was no stranger to hardship and privation. Electrician's Mate 3rd Class Curtis Rudolph Cockrell of Shreveport, Louisiana, was drinking coffee on the third deck with his fellow "electrical friends" when Admiral Byrd appeared at the hatch and remarked on the smell of the coffee. Cockrell washed him a cup and started to pour, when Byrd stopped him and said he could pour his own. He sat with the men for a while, discussing, as Cockrell remembered, their "thoughts and feelings." He asked if he could return to have coffee with them again, and he did in fact come back several times. Cockrell remembered him as "the most down to earth and congenial high ranking officer I had ever met."

As Byrd first stepped aboard, Seaman 2nd Class John Roy Haughee of Rockville, Indiana, stepped back and brought the broom he had been using to sweep away water "to attention." The admiral smiled as he passed. Later, Byrd appeared where Haughee and others were drinking coffee and asked for a cup. When told all the cups were dirty, Byrd's rejoinder was a simple "I've drunk from dirtier cups than these. Pour me a cup."

A vignette shared by Seaman 1st Class Jack Ervin Schooley of Southmont, Pennsylvania, was the most powerful of all. Schooley was in the line at the "gedunk" (ice cream stand and soda fountain) when two officers exercised what must have been the routine privilege of cutting to the front of the line. Byrd ordered them to go the end of the line, just as he had done. They complied.

Admiral Richard E. Byrd during World War II. (NARA)

Byrd remained on board *Alabama* for three weeks, until 8 August 1945, when he transferred first to the destroyer *Ault* (DD-698) and then to the aircraft carrier USS *Essex*, all still off the east coast of Honshu. He had made a lasting impression on the enlisted members of the crew for his humility, friendliness, and approachability.

ALABAMA'S COMBAT OPERATIONS AND VOYAGES

INITIAL DEPLOYMENT

Alabama steamed from Hampton Roads into Chesapeake Bay on 11 November 1942 to begin her lengthy shakedown period. She accomplished such necessary preliminary work as calibrating her degaussing system, which decreased the magnetic field around the ship and reduced the chances of detonating a magnetically triggered mine or torpedo nearby.

She first entered the Atlantic Ocean proper on 19 November in the company of two destroyers. Her crew calculated her displacement at 40,500 tons, with a mean draft of 32 feet 5 inches. She returned the next day to the Norfolk Navy Yard for the remainder of the month.

For the entire month of December 1942 *Alabama* was either in the Chesapeake, at Norfolk, or anchored just offshore in Hampton Roads or Annapolis Roads. One memorable experience (harrowing for Captain Wilson but amusing in retrospect for the crew) occurred when *Alabama* become lodged on a sandbar in the Chesapeake. The entire crew was ordered to line up on one side of the ship and run in unison to the other, in order to induce a rocking motion that might free the ship. The ploy failed, and tugboats had to do the job. There appear to have been no adverse effects on Captain Wilson's career from the incident.

Alabama's first extended voyage commenced just before the new year; she left Hampton Roads on 27 December and arrived at Casco Bay, Maine, off Portland, on 30 December. She operated near Casco Bay for nearly two weeks, conducting extensive advanced battle practice, firing the main and secondary batteries

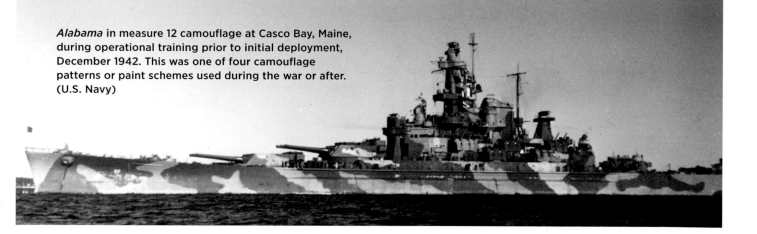

***Alabama* in measure 12 camouflage at Casco Bay, Maine, during operational training prior to initial deployment, December 1942. This was one of four camouflage patterns or paint schemes used during the war or after. (U.S. Navy)**

and catapulting her planes to serve as spotters. She returned to Norfolk on 16 January and spent ten days in dry dock there before returning to Casco Bay for the entire month of March 1943. This shakedown period completed successfully, revealing and remediating operational deficiencies, *Alabama* was now ready for her first combat deployment—to the North Atlantic.

The Battle of the Atlantic had been under way since long before the United States joined World War II. Germany's naval and air forces had been remarkably successful in sinking a large quantity of merchant shipping headed to Britain. Germany's efforts had been so profitable, in fact, that American and British planners experienced serious doubts about whether Britain could endure, since that island held far more people than could be supported with its own resources and agricultural production. One of the major reasons Hitler gleefully joined Japan in its war on the United States was to be able to unleash fully German submarines (U-boats) on all U.S. merchant shipping and naval escorts which, since the summer of 1941, had been engaged in a limited shooting war against the German submarines.

Alabama's role was not directly in an antisubmarine capacity; indeed, she herself required destroyer escorts to find and neutralize submarines that threatened her. *Alabama* could, however, provide antiaircraft fire for the ships of her formation (see "Antiaircraft Defense in the *South Dakota*–Class Battleships" on page 36), and, much more importantly, she could swing into surface action should German battleships attempt to strike convoys. Most particularly, the German battleship *Tirpitz*, based in Norwegian fjords, had emerged from time to time to menace shipping and escorts bound for the Soviet Union's port of Murmansk. Because of fuel shortages and the danger of British air attacks outside the heavily protected fjords, *Tirpitz* as it turned out would remain anchored the entire time *Alabama* was steaming in the North Atlantic in defense of convoys.

The initial stop on this deployment was Placentia Bay in Newfoundland, Canada, for most of April and the first part of May 1943. On 12 May, in the company of her sister battleship *South Dakota*, *Alabama* stood out from Placentia Bay bound for the open waters of the North Atlantic as part of Task Force 61. The task force zigzagged to guard against torpedo attack, but none came. *Alabama* suffered her first loss of life in a combat zone at this time: Fireman 3rd Class Wilburn Alvin Manning Jr. of Culverton, Georgia, was reported missing on 15 April, only minutes after he had stopped to chat with Bob Feller (see "Hall of Fame Baseball Pitcher Bob Feller Remember His Service," on page 66). The destroyer *Fitch* (DD-462) searched for Manning for an hour and a half, but since the formation was moving in darkness to avoid revealing its location to German submarines, it was a hopeless task. Manning was presumed to have fallen overboard and declared lost.

The crew on board at the time would remember the freezing conditions in the North Atlantic as strongly

The war diary entry reflecting the loss overboard of Fireman 3rd Class Wilburn Alvin Manning Jr. in the North Atlantic. (NARA)

Clearing the deck of ice in the North Atlantic in 1943. (U.S. Navy)

as they would any other shared experience during the war. They were allowed to grow beards, and personnel on watch outside sometimes served shifts limited to 20 minutes at a time. They wore felt liners in their boots, along with ski pants and face masks (with closeable mouth flaps that would allow them to smoke during daylight hours).

Alabama steamed first to Scapa Flow (the British naval base in the Orkney Islands) and assumed duty as part of the British Home Fleet, under the command of a British admiral, Bruce Fraser, on board HMS *Duke of York*. The Home Fleet was guarding against not only the appearance of *Tirpitz* but also a sortie by the battlecruiser *Scharnhorst*. But *Scharnhorst* too was hobbled by fuel shortages and other issues at this time and did not challenge any formation of which *Alabama* was a part.

The Home Fleet dispatched *Alabama* in June and July 1943 as part of various forces to Iceland, including, on 7 June 1943, to a position above the Arctic Circle (allowing her crew to boast of becoming members of the Order of the Blue Nose). Their northernmost recorded position was close to Bear Island in the Barents Sea, north of latitude 73, on 11 June. While these waters had seen attacks on convoys, none materialized on this occasion, and *Alabama* steamed with her formation for Iceland. She anchored at Hvalfjörður on 13 June and steamed back to Scapa Flow on 19 June, arriving on

Alabama at Scapa Flow, 1943. (U.S. Navy)

Alabama in Iceland in 1943. (U.S. Navy)

the 21st. Her task group remained there for over two weeks before once again making the trip to Hvalfjörður.

Her return to Scapa Flow from Iceland this final time would lead to something more dramatic, especially in the memory of the crew. She was assigned to Operation Governor, a feint toward Norway intended to focus German attention on the North Sea at a time when major Allied operations were under way in the Mediterranean around Sicily. For four days at the end of July the ships of the Home Fleet attempted to draw out *Tirpitz*, although *Alabama* was always stationed very close to Iceland.

This was her last operation in the North Atlantic. *Alabama* received orders to return to Norfolk for a brief overhaul, including time in dry dock. She arrived there on 9 August 1943 and departed for the Panama Canal on the 21st, again accompanied by her sister battleship *South Dakota*.

Painting of *Alabama* as part of Operation Governor, July 1943, by Dwight Shepler, USNR. (U.S. Navy)

Alabama stands out from the Norfolk Navy Yard, 20 August 1943, after ten days of limited overhaul and repair. (NHHC)

Alabama passes through the locks of the Panama Canal. (U.S. Navy)

ALABAMA AT ANCHOR, MOORED, OR DRY-DOCKED, NOVEMBER 1942–DECEMBER 1945

Alabama was anchored, moored, or dry-docked in or at the listed place at least once during the indicated month. If, for instance, she stood out from an anchorage and returned to it later the same month, only one entry has been recorded. When she remained in a given location into a new month, an entry is given for each month, even if Alabama did not get under way.

November 1942	Norfolk Navy Yard, Virginia	December 1943	Espiritu Santo, New Hebrides
December 1942	Chesapeake Bay		Efate, New Hebrides
	Hampton Roads, Virginia	January 1944	Efate, New Hebrides
	Norfolk Naval Operating Base, Virginia		Pearl Harbor, Hawaii (dry-docked)
	Annapolis Roads, Maryland		Funafuti
	Norfolk Navy Yard, Virginia	February 1944	Majuro, Marshall Islands
	Casco Bay, Maine	March 1944	Majuro, Marshall Islands
January 1943	Casco Bay, Maine	April 1944	Majuro, Marshall Islands
	Norfolk Navy Yard, Virginia (dry-docked)	May 1944	Majuro, Marshall Islands
		June 1944	Majuro, Marshall Islands
February 1943	Norfolk Navy Yard, Virginia	July 1944	Eniwetok, Marshall Islands
	Hampton Roads, Virginia	August 1944	Eniwetok, Marshall Islands
	Norfolk Naval Operating Base, Virginia	September 1944	Saipan, Mariana Islands
	Casco Bay, Maine	October 1944	Ulithi, Caroline Islands
March 1943	Casco Bay, Maine	November 1944	Ulithi, Caroline Islands
April 1943	Placentia Bay, Argentia, Newfoundland	December 1944	Ulithi, Caroline Islands
		January 1945	Pearl Harbor, Hawaii
May 1943	Scapa Flow, Orkney Islands, Scotland	February 1945	Navy Yard, Puget Sound, Washington (dry-docked)
June 1943	Hvalfjörður, Iceland	March 1945	Orchard Point, Washington
	Eyjafjörður, Iceland		Sinclair Inlet, Puget Sound, Washington
	Scapa Flow, Orkney Islands, Scotland		San Pedro, California
July 1943	Hvalfjörður, Iceland	April 1945	Pearl Harbor, Hawaii
	Scapa Flow, Orkney Islands, Scotland		Ulithi, Caroline Islands
		May 1945	Ulithi, Caroline Islands
August 1943	Norfolk Navy Yard, Virginia (dry-docked)	June 1945	San Pedro Bay, Leyte Gulf, Philippines
	Balboa, Panama Canal Zone	September 1945	Tokyo Bay, Japan
September 1943	Efate, New Hebrides		Buckner Bay, Okinawa (Nakagusuku Bay)
October 1943	Efate, New Hebrides	October 1945	San Francisco, California
November 1943	Nandi, Fiji		San Pedro, California
		November 1945	San Pedro, California
		December 1945	San Pedro, California

BATTLE STAR 1: GILBERT ISLANDS, NOVEMBER–DECEMBER 1943

During World War II, U.S. Navy ships were awarded commendations, usually referred to as "battle stars," to mark their participation in combat operations. Alabama *received a total of nine battle stars for her engagements in the Pacific.*

By the time *Alabama* joined combat operations in the Pacific, it had been nearly two years since the Japanese attack on Pearl Harbor. Success had come for the United States at sea in such great naval battles in the Pacific as the ones in the Coral Sea (May 1942), at Midway (June 1942), and near Guadalcanal (November 1942). But on land, progress had been limited to portions of New Guinea and some of the Solomon Islands, including Guadalcanal itself.

While General Douglas MacArthur led U.S. and Allied forces through New Guinea toward the Philippines, the U.S. Navy's Chief of Naval Operations, Admiral Ernest King, wanted to employ the U.S. Pacific Fleet and Marine Corps in a series of attacks far to MacArthur's north and east. These offensives would initiate the Central Pacific drive that the U.S. Navy had long foreseen as the route toward a victory over Japan. Admiral Chester W. Nimitz, commander-in-chief of the Pacific Fleet, was ordered by the U.S. Joint Chiefs of Staff to plan and execute an attack on the Japanese-held Gilbert Islands in November 1943, code-named Operation Galvanic.

The Japanese had seized the Gilberts shortly after their attack on Pearl Harbor. The main U.S. objective of Galvanic was the airfield on the island of Betio in Tarawa Atoll. Two nearby atolls, Makin and Abemama, were also included. U.S. Marines and soldiers of the U.S. Army were to be landed to destroy Japanese defenses and occupy the islands.

Alabama did not participate directly in the amphibious assaults. As one of the new fast battleships, her place would be with the aircraft carriers that were to guard against the very real threat that Japan would sortie its fleet from Truk in the Caroline Islands or forces from the even closer Marshall Islands to attempt to defeat the landings in the Gilberts. *Alabama* spent the days and nights while ground fighting was under way at Tarawa and Makin patrolling with USS *Yorktown* (CV-10), USS *Lexington* (CV-16), and USS *Cowpens* (CVL-25) north of Makin Atoll. U.S. carrier aircraft from this group attacked Japanese bases on Mili and Jaluit Atolls, the closest of the Marshall Islands to the Gilberts, and prevented coordinated interference with the landings. *Alabama*'s chief role was to provide antiaircraft fire, if needed, for the carriers and to be ready for surface action should Japanese battleships or cruisers emerge. But they didn't.

After the landings in the Gilberts were deemed successful on 23 November 1943, *Alabama* remained east of Tarawa for a number of days to help cover the withdrawal of troop transports, hospital ships, and cargo ships to Pearl Harbor. She had two occasions in this period to fire on Japanese aircraft. On 27 November a Betty bomber appeared suddenly out of the fog at an altitude of 1,200 feet, apparently as surprised to see *Alabama* as the American sailors were to see the bomber. The 40-mm and 20-mm guns fired briefly, falling silent as the plane disappeared again, likely unscathed. On 28 November, all her 5-inch/38 mounts on the port side fired for two minutes at a plane some 8,500 yards distant and were joined by one of the 40-mm quad emplacements. This plane too seems to have escaped.

On 6 December 1943, *Alabama* moved south of

Alabama, just to the left of the light carrier Monterey (CVL-26), approaching the Gilbert Islands during Operation Galvanic. (U.S. Navy)

The Nauru bombardment of 8 December 1943. (U.S. Navy)

Tarawa and then steamed west toward the Japanese-held island of Nauru, a phosphate-mining site important for Japan's war effort. On the 8th, along with the fast battleships *Indiana*, *Massachusetts*, *North Carolina*, *South Dakota*, and *Washington* and the carriers *Bunker Hill* (CV-17) and *Monterey* (CVL-26), *Alabama* bombarded Nauru. The force laid waste to its facilities. *Alabama* expended 135 rounds of 16-inch and 400 rounds of 5-inch fire, hitting barracks, power facilities, antiaircraft emplacements, the airfield, and fuel storage sites.

Upon completing these, her first main-battery salvos of the war fired in anger, *Alabama* steamed for the U.S. naval base at Espiritu Santo in the New Hebrides before heading for Pearl Harbor in January 1944 and a brief stay in a dry dock to replace one of her propellers.

BATTLE STAR 2: MARSHALL ISLANDS, JANUARY–FEBRUARY 1944

Admiral Nimitz was ordered to use the captured Gilbert Islands as a springboard for his sailors, soldiers, and attacking the Marshall Islands in January 1944. A series of widely scattered coral atolls, the Marshalls were a logical step on the way to the Mariana Islands, which were to become the major U.S. objective in the Central Pacific in 1944.

Prior to World War I, the Marshalls had been German colonial possessions. Japan seized the islands during that war, and the League of Nations mandated them to Japan. Japan had plenty of time to fortify and man bases in the isolated atolls without close observation by any other world power. The islands' obscurity made them dangerous to the United States, a peril that led to the decision to attack Tarawa and the other Gilberts first, in order to have nearby air bases from which to fly reconnaissance and bombing missions against the Marshalls.

Once the Marshalls had been taken, air bases for similar missions against Japanese holdings farther west would be in hand. In addition, the Marshalls' larger atolls could serve as forward anchorages from which the U.S. fleet could stage future assaults far closer to the intended targets and to repair and resupply ships without requiring them to return to Pearl Harbor.

Code-named Operation Flintlock, the action involved: (1) the seizure of Majuro Atoll, which was known to be essentially undefended by the Japanese; (2) the attack on Kwajalein Atoll, which held the major concentration of Japanese forces in the Marshalls on three of its islands (Roi, Namur, and Kwajalein); and (3) the assault on Eniwetok Atoll, one of the westernmost of the Marshalls. *Alabama* was assigned to Task Group 58.2, along with *North Carolina* and *South Dakota*. There was little need for the battleships' potent antiaircraft fire, since preliminary raids by U.S. carrier aircraft had wiped out all Japanese shore-based aircraft and the Japanese fleet did not emerge to contest the landings in the Marshalls. Not a single U.S. ship would be damaged by aircraft during this operation.

Alabama would contribute by using her main and secondary batteries at Kwajalein to bombard the adjacent islands of Roi and Namur on 30 January 1944, in preparation for the landings there by U.S. Marines on 1 February. *Alabama* fired 276 rounds of high-capacity ammunition and 45 armor-piercing projectiles from her 16-inch guns. She used radar to "spot" (correct) the fire. Among the chief targets were reinforced concrete blockhouses of the sort that had proved impervious to naval bombardments at Tarawa, and the results this time were little better, at least as far as *Alabama* was concerned. None of her high-capacity rounds damaged the blockhouses, and the armor-piercing rounds did not appear to score direct hits.

Still, the fire from all U.S. warships and aircraft was sufficient to enable far more successful and safe landings for the Marines at Roi and Namur than had been the case in the

Gilberts. Most of Alabama's fire was at ranges between 8,000 and 12,000 yards, although some rounds were from both longer and shorter distances. Her secondary battery of 5-inch guns fired 1,562 rounds at Roi and Namur.

With her bombardment in support of initial landings complete, *Alabama* moved with her task group first west of Kwajalein and then quickly to the new fleet anchorage at recently captured Majuro Atoll. On 11 February she sortied in support of one of the most audacious raids of the middle part of the war: the attempt to catch the Japanese fleet by surprise at its anchorage in Truk Lagoon in the Caroline Islands.

BATTLE STAR 3: ASIATIC-PACIFIC RAIDS, FEBRUARY–MAY 1944

With the quick success of the invasions of Kwajalein and Majuro and mounting signs that the Japanese were reinforcing their defenses on the next planned American objective in the Marshalls (Eniwetok Atoll), Nimitz and the Central Pacific force commander, Vice Admiral Raymond A. Spruance, decided to accelerate the schedule for that assault. But to do so would be risky under the prevailing circumstances, since Eniwetok was only 750 miles from the major Japanese naval base at Truk Lagoon in the Caroline Islands. It would be essential first to neutralize Truk to prevent any interference with landings at Eniwetok.

Truk was the base of the Japanese Combined Fleet, as well as a major submarine base and staging point for their operations throughout the Central Pacific. For much of the war the flagship of the Combined Fleet, the superbattleship *Musashi*, had been stationed there. Although the Japanese had become aware of the vulnerability of Truk and had withdrawn most major ships before the U.S. attack on the Marshalls

USS *ALABAMA* MAIN BATTERY, ROUNDS EXPENDED IN COMBAT, 1943–1945

DATE	LOCATION	ROUNDS FIRED
8 December 1943	Nauru	135
30 January 1944	Roi and Namur, Kwajalein Atoll	321
1 May 1944	Ponape	84
13 June 1944	Saipan	360
10 June 1945	Minami Daito Jima	81
17 July 1945	Honshu	271
TOTAL		1,252

Japanese ships after being attacked in Truk Lagoon, 17 February 1944. (NARA)

commenced, the remaining Japanese forces there were a potential irritant to U.S. operations in the Marshalls and Marianas.

Any successful attack on Truk would have to come from aircraft launched from carriers. The heart of the lagoon at Truk was simply too distant from the open sea to allow a successful attack from even the biggest guns of U.S. battleships. So, once again, *Alabama*'s role would be in support of carrier operations. While the carrier planes executed devastating attacks on the few Japanese warships and supply vessels still at Truk, *Alabama* provided antiaircraft screening for the carriers over 100 miles east of the lagoon.

After the attack on Truk, *Alabama* steamed about 700 miles to the northwest with Task Force 58 to the vicinity of the Mariana Islands. Aircraft from carriers launched attacks on Japanese ground positions on the islands of Saipan, Tinian, and Guam. *Alabama* provided antiaircraft support for the carriers, and this time there would be no lack of opportunities for it, since the task force was close to major Japanese airbases on the Marianas. *Alabama* was part of Task Group (TG) 58.2, whose task was to screen the carriers *Essex*, *Yorktown*, and *Belleau Wood* (CVL-24), alongside the battleship

South Dakota and the light cruisers *Santa Fe* (CL-60), *Mobile* (CL-63), *Biloxi* (CL-80), and *Oakland* (CL-95).

On 22 February 1944, the task group sighted one Japanese Val dive-bomber, one Tony fighter, and 20 to 24 Betty bombers. The planes approached TG 58.2 in groups of four to six, then split off to make individual attacks some ten to 12 miles out. Thanks to the heavy, accurate fire from the screening ships, including *Alabama*, none of the Japanese planes succeeded in damaging any U.S. vessels. *Alabama* herself shot down three Betty bombers on torpedo runs: one by 5-inch/38-caliber fire, a second with 40-mm guns; and a third with a combination of 20-mm and 40-mm fire.

Earlier during this operation, *Alabama* had suffered her only combat-related fatalities of the war, although not from enemy fire. During a lull in Japanese air attacks, at 2300 on 21 February, the Mount 9, the aftmost twin-barrel 5-inch/38-caliber mount in a row of guns on the upper level of the starboard side, fired two rounds into the back of the nearest of those guns, Mount 5 (see "Mount 5 Accident" box on the next page).

After operations near the Marianas had concluded, *Alabama* returned to Majuro Atoll in the Marshall Islands for four weeks at anchor, repairs to Mount 5, and resupply.

UNITED STATES NAVAL INSTITUTE

Alabama next sortied from Majuro on 22 March, bound for the Palau Islands, 2,500 miles to the west. She was a part of Task Group 58.9, commanded by Vice Admiral Willis A. Lee on board North Carolina, as part of Task Force 58, commanded by Vice Admiral Marc A. Mitscher on board Lexington. En route, the newly repaired Mount 5 was test-fired on 23 March.

As the task force approached the Palaus on 29 March 1944, it was attacked by numerous Japanese planes 250 miles southeast of those islands. Alabama fired her 5-inch/38-caliber guns at two Betty bombers passing by at 7,000 yards on the starboard side. One of the Bettys burst into flames and crashed, while the other escaped. Alabama continued her screening the next day as the carriers launched attacks on the Palau Islands. That evening, shortly after dark, another wave of attacking Japanese bombers approached the formation. As the planes grew ever closer, all three types of antiaircraft guns on board Alabama engaged them. But neither the planes nor the ships appear to have been struck during the encounter.

On 31 March 1944, as the Palaus were being hit yet again by U.S. aircraft, Alabama catapulted two planes into the air in a fruitless search for pilots downed over the islands. After a final day of air strikes on 1 April, the task force turned to the east for the long voyage back to Majuro, which it reached on 6 April. Alabama would remain there for only a week, after which she would depart for the first time for waters off New Guinea.

The Mount 5 Accident

Late in the evening of 21 February 1944, Alabama was steaming as part of a circular antiaircraft formation approximately 360 miles east of Saipan. South Dakota was off the formation's port flank, Alabama off the starboard. Their 5-inch/38 guns would be the mainstays of any defense of their formation against likely nighttime attacks by aircraft launching torpedoes. It was nearly a new moon, so the sky was dark, as were the ships themselves.

At 2255 Alabama's search radar detected three unidentified aircraft, "bogies," heading toward the formation from the west. The 5-inch gun mounts were fully manned with crews of 13 each. The training of the mounts and the elevation of their guns was to be determined from data acquired by the fire-control directors and fed to the Mark 1A computer in the plotting room, which would send signals to the mounts that positioned their guns correctly.

As Alabama sought to fire accurately at nearby Japanese aircraft, Captain Kirtland ordered the ship to turn to starboard. Since the targets then being tracked had been off the starboard side at 10,000 yards, the gun mounts began training toward the ship's bow in order to remain pointed at them. Past a certain point in this rotation, of course, the guns would be pointed at some portion of the ship, possibly even at one of the neighboring gun mounts. This is precisely what happened: Mount 9, the pair of guns farthest aft among the five two-barrel mounts on the starboard side, rotated until it pointed directly into the back of its neighbor on superstructure level 02, Mount 5.

As to what came next, there is disagreement between the official record and memories of many of the enlisted men who had personal knowledge of events that night. Captain Kirtland's report, dated 24 February 1944, stated that the guns "went into the stops"—that is, they turned so far that they engaged automatic devices meant to prevent firing at the ship's structure.

Kirtland reported that an experienced member of the crew in Mount 9 decided, for inexplicable reasons, that the guns should be fired anyway and, employing a work-around, released a clutch lever that permitted firing. But several enlisted men later recalled hearing someone, perhaps an officer, insisting over a sound-operated telephone circuit that the guns had to be cleared immediately. The voice allegedly repeated the point multiple times until someone in Mount 9 responded by firing.

Whatever the case, both guns fired, and the consequences were deadly. One of the rounds struck directly in the center top of the back plate of Mount 5, on the other side of which the mount captain, Gunner's Mate 2nd Class David Pinckney Leopard Jr. of Newberry, South Carolina, was stationed. Leopard was essentially obliterated by the blast. A second round, from Mount 9's left gun, punched through the top left of Mount 5's rear plating. Three other members of the Mount 5 crew were killed: Seaman 2nd Class Albert Dale Roberts of Pink, West Virginia; Gunner's Mate 3rd Class Matthew Trojan of Linfield, Pennsylvania; and Seaman 1st Class Manuel Rodrigues Vegas of San Francisco, California.

Standing nearby outside Mount 5, Steward's Mate 1st Class Robert Lee Langston of Norfolk, Virginia, was struck in the thigh by at least one shard of metal. He too would succumb. In addition to these 5 deaths, 11 men were wounded, some of them gravely, with second- and third-degree burns, broken limbs, and shell-fragment injuries.

The exact cause of the accident remains a mystery. On 1 March 1944, the commander of Alabama's Task Unit 58.2.2 and Battleship Division 9, Rear Admiral Edward W. Hanson, convened a court of inquiry on board Alabama while she was anchored at Majuro one week after the accident. After tireless searching, naval historian Jared Galloway discovered that the official record of the proceeding, at one time held and catalogued by the Navy's Office of the Judge Advocate General, was missing from the archives. Thus whatever documentation from the hearing that might tell us the cause of the accident more precisely is, at least for now, absent. The sight-setter blamed by Kirtland for initiating the accident remained unnamed and was apparently transferred from the ship without testifying at the hearing.

In the early 1980s, veterans of Alabama's 5th Division, to which Mount 5's crew was assigned, initiated a campaign to commemorate the accident and their lost comrades. They secured the permission of the Battleship Alabama Memorial Commission to attach a bronze plaque to the back of the repaired Mount 5 listing the last names and initials of those who died. They were the only members of the crew of the otherwise "Lucky A" to die in a combat-related incident during the war. The plaque, affixed in April 1985, now reminds all visitors of this poignant loss.

Burial at sea of the dead from the Mount 5 accident, 22 February 1944. (U.S. Navy)

Funeral ceremony for the dead from the Mount 5 accident, 22 February 1944. (U.S. Navy)

Mount 9, right, fired into the back of Mount 5, left, as both were pointed toward the bow of the ship. A plaque on the back of Mount 5 honors the fallen (museum configuration). (Daniel Rogers)

BATTLE STAR 4: HOLLANDIA, APRIL 1944

After a week at anchor at Majuro Atoll, from 6 to 13 April 1944, *Alabama* steamed 2,200 miles to the southwest with Task Group 58.3, led by Rear Admiral John W. Reeves Jr. in USS *Enterprise* (CV-6). The goal was an area at sea off the north-central coast of New Guinea. *Alabama* would support an amphibious attack by forces under the command of General MacArthur to push the Japanese back from strongholds on the world's second-largest island.

In March 1944, the Joint Chiefs of Staff had ordered MacArthur and Nimitz to collaborate in an operation, code-named Reckless, to occupy territory at Hollandia, just over the border in Dutch New Guinea from the Australian-administered eastern portion of the island. Since early 1942, Hollandia had been occupied, as had much of the northern coast of island, by Japanese troops. Australian and U.S. forces had succeeded, both on land and at sea (most notably at the Battle of the Coral Sea in May 1942), in preventing the Japanese from spilling around the southeastern tip of New Guinea at Milne Bay or landing at Port Moresby on the southeastern coast. Throughout 1942 and 1943, these Allied forces assaulted and "leapfrogged" (bypassed and left cut off) Japanese positions along the northeastern coast of New Guinea. Now in April 1944 at Hollandia, MacArthur, supported by Nimitz's fleet, would attack and seize the only good anchorage on the northern coast, at Humboldt Bay.

A preliminary air raid on 30 March had all but wiped out Japanese air forces in the area. There were only two remaining threats: air attacks from the Vogelkop Peninsula in extreme northwestern New Guinea or the Palau Islands, and naval interference by the Japanese Combined Fleet. The Japanese decided, however, not to risk their fleet in this action and left the men they had sent to Hollandia to fight and die without any further support.

Task Force 58, including *Alabama*, arrived off the coast of Hollandia on 21 April and launched air attacks on the bases that had already been wiped out by the bombing runs on 30 March. They met, of course, little resistance. No Japanese planes rose to challenge the Americans. No U.S. ships were damaged by enemy fire. *Alabama*, ready to protect the carriers or even engage surface ships that might have appeared, did not have to fire its guns.

As something of a consolation for not being able to fire on Japanese aircraft or ships, on its way back Task Force 58 targeted the two Japanese strongholds of Truk and Ponape, between Hollandia and the Marshalls. (Technically, the operations against Truk and Ponape were recognized by *Alabama*'s third battle star, as part of the Asiatic-Pacific Raids of 1944, although they occurred *after* the actions at Hollandia, for which she received her fourth star).

First, the carriers again struck at Truk on 30 April 1944. Once more, *Alabama* and the other battleships served as a screen but did not fire at any enemy forces on land, at sea, or in the air. The next day, however, the six battleships—*Alabama, Iowa, Massachusetts, New Jersey, North Carolina,* and *South Dakota*—were turned loose as Task Group 58.7 in a bombardment of the island of Ponape, 420 miles east of Truk. On this island the Japanese had completed a seaplane base and an airfield and were building another airfield. *Alabama* fired 84 high-capacity rounds during the 78-minute operation: 45 at Ponape town, and 39 at two smaller islands. Her targets were coastal-defense guns, antiaircraft positions, and buildings. The secondary battery (five-inch) fired 286 rounds during the furious bombardment, which Task Group 58.7 commander Vice Admiral Lee halted when he surmised no good targets remained and further fire would be a waste of ammunition.

Alabama returned to Majuro to prepare for her role in what would be the biggest operation in the Pacific to date, the invasion of the Mariana Islands.

BATTLE STAR 5: MARIANAS OPERATION, JUNE–AUGUST 1944

Ever since the U.S. Joint Chiefs of Staff and the U.S./ British Combined Chiefs of Staff had approved a drive through the Central Pacific, beginning in the Gilbert Islands, an invasion of the Mariana Islands had been likely. These islands included Guam, which had been a U.S. territory since the Spanish-American War but had been lost to Japan in December 1941. Guam and the Japanese island of Saipan would make good forward naval bases for the next step toward Japan, whatever that step might be. Also, Tinian and Saipan were excellent sites for air bases for the new B-29 Superfortress bomber, which would be capable of reaching the Japanese home islands from there.

After taking the Marianas, the United States could attack in a number of different directions: toward the Bonin Islands (including Iwo Jima) to the north, the

Philippines to the west, Formosa to the northwest, or the Palau Islands (including Peleliu) to the southwest. Once holding the Marianas, moreover, the United States could complicate Japanese resupply of such formerly important bases as the ones at Truk and New Guinea.

It is a measure of how far the United States had come, and how fast, that in June 1944, only two and a half years after the attack on Pearl Harbor, it could attack both the Marianas (in Operation Forager) and France (Operation Overlord) simultaneously. In Forager, *Alabama* would be a part of the largest fleet operation of the Pacific war to date. Over 500 ships and 127,000 troops would participate.

After the operations at Hollandia, Truk, and Ponape of late April and early May, *Alabama* remained at anchor at Majuro from 4 May until 6 June 1944. She then sortied with Task Group 58.7 (consisting of battleships, cruisers, and destroyers) but once under way would be detached to Task Group 58.3 (dominated by three aircraft carriers) and become part of a mighty antiaircraft screening force. Upon reaching the vicinity

of Saipan on 13 June, *Alabama* rejoined Task Group 58.7, which consisted of Battleship Divisions 7 and 9, numerous destroyers, and USS *Indianapolis* (CA-35), the flagship of the commander of the Fifth Fleet, Admiral Spruance. *Alabama*, *South Dakota*, and their escorts detached from the main group to bombard Saipan in support of an amphibious assault by Marines and soldiers that would begin on 15 June.

On 13 June, *Alabama* fired 360 rounds from her main battery of 16-inch guns and 1,763 from her 5-inch guns. The main-battery rounds were high-capacity shells fired with reduced charges. The targets included coastal-defense, dual-purpose, and field artillery, as well as ammunition storage and warehouses. *Alabama* reported doing great damage to the main town of Garapan. She received almost no Japanese fire, only a few rounds from a damaged ship in Garapan Harbor. However, because the new fast battleships had had little practice or experience firing at targets in support of upcoming amphibious assaults (*Alabama*'s only other such attack had been at Roi and Namur at Kwajalein

The bombardment of Saipan, June 1944. (NARA)

UNITED STATES NAVAL INSTITUTE

in the Marshall Islands), the results were not as good as first reported. Nor were they as impressive as those achieved in the next day's bombardment from the more seasoned old battleships, whose primary function all along had been to support landing operations.

Alabama's greatest service to the American war effort during this momentous week would come not from her main guns but from her air-search radar and Combat Information Center. After the invasion of Saipan was under way, Admiral Spruance received messages from U.S. submarines stationed off the Philippines that a major Japanese naval force was entering the Philippine Sea and heading toward Saipan. The Japanese navy was executing its A-Go Plan to engage the U.S. Navy in a decisive fleet operation. Its aim was to destroy enough

of the U.S. Navy to shatter American morale and force a negotiated peace that would allow Japan to keep its conquests from earlier in the war. Spruance ordered his aircraft carriers and fast battleships, including *Alabama*, to steam west under Vice Admiral Lee to meet the onrushing Japanese fleet. Meanwhile, the Japanese were searching for Task Force 58. They found it early on the morning of 19 June and launched aircraft to attack.

At 1006, *Alabama* reported to Lee that her radar had detected "a large bogie," or an unidentified group of aircraft, 141 miles west of her position (see "To *Alabama*, Very Well Done" on page 87). The early warning from *Alabama* enabled the commander of Task Force 58, Vice Admiral Mitscher, to vector Hellcat fighters to the Japanese planes organizing themselves for

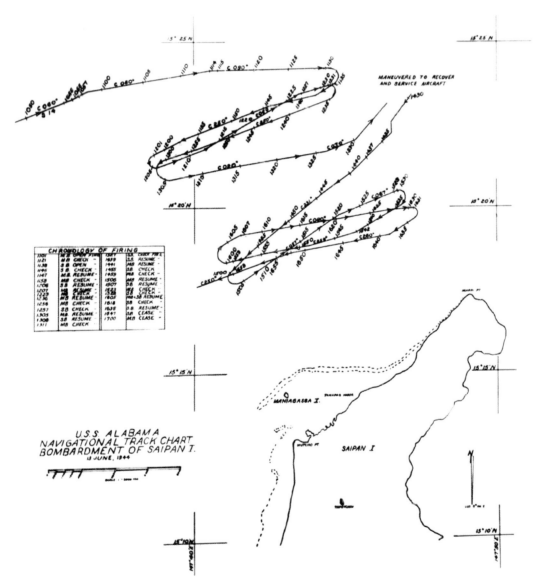

Sketch from the after-action report by USS *Alabama* on the bombardment of Saipan, 12 June 1944, showing the ship's track as she was firing. (NARA)

Four admirals important in USS *Alabama*'s story (from left to right): Raymond A. Spruance, Marc A. Mitscher, Chester W. Nimitz, and Willis A. Lee. (U.S. Navy)

the attack. The Hellcats struck the Japanese planes 70 miles from the U.S. fleet. Thus began the elimination of Japanese naval aviation in an action soon known as "The Great Marianas Turkey Shoot."

Some Japanese bombers did survive to push forward to the ships screening the carriers, including *Alabama*. At 1047, *Alabama*'s five-inch guns, directed by Sky 3, the starboard antiaircraft fire director, opened fire. During this first attack, one Japanese dive-bomber struck the nearby battleship *South Dakota*. Over the next hours, *Alabama*'s 5-inch, 40-mm, and 20-mm guns fired at numerous attacking Japanese planes. One torpedo passed several hundred yards astern of her. A dive-bomber succeeded in approaching *Alabama* undetected, passed over her from the starboard bow to the port quarter, and dropped two small bombs, one of which hit only 100 feet away. Shortly thereafter, the *Alabama* crew witnessed a crashing Japanese torpedo bomber carom off the sea surface and strike *Indiana*.

Alabama's radar provided reports throughout the engagement on very distant Japanese planes forming

up for new raids. *Alabama* fired a total of 428 5-inch antiaircraft shells during the day, along with 1,228 rounds of 40-mm ammunition and 611 of 20-mm. By the end of the day she had assisted in the downing of only one Japanese plane, but her search radar antennas over 100 feet above the waterline had been one of the most important, if unheralded, participants in the Battle of the Philippine Sea.

The next day, 20 June 1944, the carriers that *Alabama* screened participated in one of the most dramatic scenes of the entire Pacific war. Mitscher ordered an attack on retiring Japanese carriers late in the afternoon, at the extreme range of the U.S. aircraft. Many of those aircraft would go down at sea when they ran out of fuel, and others were able to land safely in the darkness only because Mitscher violated standard practice by lighting up the carriers and nearby ships in order to guide them home.

In the coming days, *Alabama* would steam to the vicinity of Saipan and the other islands of the Marianas to support and protect the landed troops and help guard

Alabama's antiaircraft barrage during the Battle of the Philippine Sea, 19 June 1944. (U.S. Navy)

against renewed air attacks on U.S. carriers. She would stay in the general vicinity of Guam for most of July. The exception was a jaunt between 24 and 28 July to the Palau Islands, where she screened carriers raiding Peleliu in anticipation of an amphibious attack in September 1944.

On 11 August, after over two months at sea, *Alabama* returned to the Marshall Islands, this time to Eniwetok for three weeks at anchor. While there, on the 23rd, Captain Kirtland, widely admired by the crew as a highly effective commanding officer, was relieved by Captain Murphy.

Excerpts from "To *Alabama*, Very Well Done" *Naval History*, June 2004

By Master Chief Alvin J. Spinner, U.S. Navy (Ret.)

ALVIN JOHN SPINNER (1924–2012) SERVED ON BOARD ALABAMA THROUGHOUT WORLD WAR II AS A PROUD "PLANK OWNER," OR ORIGINAL CREW MEMBER. HE REMAINED IN THE NAVY UNTIL HIS RETIREMENT IN 1963. HERE HE RECOUNTS PRECISELY DOCUMENTED DETAILS OF ALABAMA'S ROLE IN SPOTTING THE ATTACKING JAPANESE AIRCRAFT IN THE BATTLE OF THE PHILIPPINE SEA OF JUNE 1944.

One unknown story of World War II concerns the role of the battleship USS *Alabama* (BB-60) in alerting Task Force 58 to a force of attacking enemy aircraft 60 years ago in the Battle of the Philippine Sea, commonly referred to as "The Marianas Turkey Shoot."

Historians have consistently omitted important details and circumstances of the battleship *Alabama*'s initial contact and report in June 1944. Early evidence either was disregarded or considered unsubstantiated. Today, however, with early documentation augmented by the action reports of the three on-scene Task Force 58.7 battle

line division commanders, the *Alabama*'s so-called claim finally can be substantiated.

In August 1943, a new, improved SK air-search radar was to be fitted on the *Alabama*, but because of a time constraint and the need for the two battleships of Battleship Division 9 [BatDiv 9] (the *Alabama* and *South Dakota* [BB-57]) in the Pacific, installation could not be accomplished. Thus, Captain Fred D. Kirtland had the equipment loaded aboard, with plans to install it at Pearl Harbor.

A few hours into the Pacific Ocean from the Panama Canal, Captain Kirtland announced that instead of going to Pearl Harbor, we would proceed to an advanced base at Havannah Harbor, Efate, in New Hebrides.

The ship's radar pedestal was high on the mast, about 130 feet above the waterline, with the mast extending about 30 feet higher. Normally, such installation requires use of navy-yard cranes, but *Alabama* crewmen and crewmen from a nearby repair ship muscled block-and-tackle to dismount the original air-search radar and install and calibrate the new one. This was the same radar—with the same operators—used to detect, track, and then permit reporting the approaching massive air attack force on 19 June 1944. Initially detected approximately 190 miles away, the bogie was considered by many to be an anomaly. A closing plot [successively closer ranges], the *Alabama*'s formal 1006 report at 141 miles, and then a confirmation by the battleship *Iowa* (BB-61) removed any doubt of its validity. The *South Dakota*'s description of the first attack wave at 1028, "bogey now covers an area of four miles," indicated this contact was highly unusual. . . .

. . . Selected entries from the *Alabama*'s action report chronology begin with the following:

1000—Position of *Alabama* was Latitude 14-15-55 N., Longitude 143-00-20 E. Task Group 58.7 was disposed in Cruising Disposition 7-Roger, Axis 270, Course 250, Speed 18.

1006—*Alabama* made initial contact, reporting to CTG [Commander Task Group] 58.7 a large bogie, bearing 268 true, distance 141 miles, angles 24 [subtending on the display an angle of 24 degrees] or greater, closing.

CTF 58 asked for confirmation of *Alabama*'s contact; *Iowa* substantiated. . . .

. . . Messages, originated after the Air Attacks Monday, are quoted below for information.

From CTF 58 (Vice Admiral Mitscher) to TF 58: . . . "[S]killful defense of this Task Force enabled the Force to escape a vicious well coordinated Aircraft Attack carried out with determination."

From CTG 58.7 (Vice Admiral Lee) to TG 58.7: "In the matter of reporting initial bogies, to *Iowa*, well done, to *Alabama*, very well done."

From ComBatDiv 9 (Rear Admiral Hanson) to *Alabama*: "Congratulations to you, your ship and especially to your Super Alert Radar Crew. You were in large measure responsible for yesterday's superlative Air Victory. Southwest corner was getting hot yesterday. Your help is greatly appreciated."

From *Alabama* to *South Dakota*: "All hands here express sympathy and hope casualties were light."

From *South Dakota* to *Alabama*: "Thank You. Twenty men and one officer killed. Twenty three were injured. Ten serious. One five hundred bomb struck port side at 0-1 level."

Documentation that Pacific Fleet headquarters was aware of the *Alabama*'s initial contact and considered it noteworthy appeared in U.S. Pacific Fleet, Advance Headquarters, Guam, Press Release No.182, labeled "For release at 0800 (-10), 12 August 1945." It presented brief descriptions of the *Alabama*'s participation in various operations through to 5 June 1945. But the third paragraph of page 2 reads as follows: "It was the *Alabama* which first gave the warning to the rest of her task force that a huge air-fleet of Japanese planes was approaching. The resulting battle, in which the Japanese force was turned back, has been called the first battle of the Philippines Sea. American carrier pilots termed the air battle a 'turkey shoot.'"

In a book published in 1999, containing statements by various crewmen on their memories of duty in the *Alabama*, watch officer E. Wayne Bundy commented, "In any case we got bogeys first and further out than anybody else. Turkey Shoot Day off Saipan and Guam, Joe Cook and Cliff O'Brien had incoming Japanese carrier planes so far out the Flag [i.e., Vice Admiral Lee, in his flagship Washington (BB-56)] didn't believe us. Nor our 2nd report. Nor 3rd. Finally somebody else confirmed, and they decided it was for real. (We knew that from the first blip on.)"

The radar officer, Captain (then-Lieutenant) John Henry, the two radar technical officers, (then Naval Reserve Lieutenants) Walter F. Lenoir Jr. and Eugene S. Pennebaker, and the two radar operators on watch that morning, O'Brien and Cook, were honored officially with commendations for their outstanding performance. . . .

BATTLE STAR 6: WESTERN CAROLINES, AUGUST–SEPTEMBER 1944

In September 1944, forces under the direction of Admirals Nimitz and Halsey executed an operation to attack and seize several of the western Caroline Islands. The westernmost of these are known as the Palau Islands, including Peleliu and Anguar. Japan had taken them from Germany during World War I and held them ever since as a mandate of the League of Nations. Japanese military and naval forces had constructed heavily protected airfields there, and during World War II Japan used the islands as a fleet base when it became clear that Truk was vulnerable to U.S. attacks.

In particular, the airfield on Peleliu (some 675 miles from the Philippine island of Leyte) was seen as a threat. Air forces based at Peleliu would be able to observe and harass any Allied approach to the southern portion of the Philippines from New Guinea. If, however, the airfield changed hands, the United States could use it to dominate that portion of the Pacific and to support the invasion of the Philippines. Nimitz and his top commanders began planning for an assault, under the code name Operation Stalemate II.

Alabama had already been of some assistance in developing these plans. She had screened carriers whose aircraft bombed and, more importantly, photographed the major islands of the Palau group in March and July 1944. As part of Task Force 34, *Alabama* got under way at the end of August 1944 after a three-week anchorage at Eniwetok Atoll. Under her new commanding officer, Captain Murphy, she steamed south-southwest, giving a wide berth to the bypassed Japanese positions at Ponape and Truk before turning north to approach the Palau Islands. She was steaming 170 miles west-northwest of Peleliu when on 15 September the 1st Marine Division landed on that island under heavy fire.

The task force she was screening proceeded northwest just to the east of Leyte Gulf, where planes from the carriers bombed targets in the Manila Bay area on 21 and 22 September. On 24 September, the carriers' aircraft attacked Japanese positions and shipping in central Philippines. While *Alabama* did not encounter any enemy planes or ships during this operation, she did launch one of her Kingfisher spotter aircraft in an unsuccessful effort to locate and rescue a downed American naval aviator near Mactan Island.

The Marines on Peleliu experienced some of the most brutal fighting of the Pacific war, but at least they were not hampered by major interference from the skies or seas to the west, thanks to the task force that *Alabama* screened. At the conclusion of these operations, she steamed for a one-day anchorage at Saipan, so recently taken from Japan, before heading for a new fleet anchorage at Ulithi Atoll.

BATTLE STAR 7: LEYTE OPERATION, OCTOBER–DECEMBER 1944

On 29 September 1944, after her day at anchor at Saipan, *Alabama* steamed with Task Force 34 in the direction of Ulithi Atoll in the western Caroline Islands. Ulithi had been taken from the Japanese, unopposed, by the U.S. Army's 323rd Regimental Combat Team on 22 September. For the remainder of the war, this atoll would serve as a massive, largely secret forward operating base for the Navy in the western Pacific, since it was large enough to accommodate hundreds of warships at a time. *Alabama* herself would anchor at Ulithi on four separate occasions in 1944 and 1945.

The goal of the Third Fleet's operations in this time period was to support General MacArthur's landings at Leyte in the central Philippines, scheduled to begin in earnest on 20 October. Despite strenuous arguments from the Chief of Naval Operations, Admiral King, that Formosa (Taiwan) was the only reasonable target at this point, MacArthur had won the Joint Chiefs of Staff's approval to reclaim the Philippines as the next major step in the drive to Japan. Under Admiral Halsey, the Third Fleet, of which *Alabama* was a part, would help suppress enemy air capabilities. Third Fleet would also stand ready in case the Japanese Combined Fleet chose, as it had during the Marianas operations, to sortie to precipitate a decisive battle with the Americans, one that might cripple the U.S. fleet and enable Japan to extract better terms for a peace deal.

On 3 October 1944, *Alabama* sortied from Ulithi with Task Force 34, including her fellow fast battleships *Iowa*, *Massachusetts*, *New Jersey*, *South Dakota*, and *Washington*, heading northwest toward the Ryukyu Islands, the most important of which was Okinawa. Encountering no Japanese forces, *Alabama* screened the carriers of Task Force 38 when they launched attacks on Okinawa and Kumejima.

The task force then immediately steamed due west in the direction of Formosa and the Pescadores Islands just to west. It commenced air strikes on 12 October and continued them the next day. The Japanese responded with air attacks on the task force; *Alabama* fired on numerous attacking airplanes early on 13 October and then again that same evening after dark. She expended 269 rounds from her 5-inch/38 guns during these engagements.

The Japanese attacks continued on 14 October. *Alabama* first opened fire that day at 1515, then again many times from 1710 to 1745 as well, this time at an estimated 15 to 20 Kate and Jill bombers. She claimed sole credit for downing three planes and damaging another in these attacks. She fired 202 rounds of 5-inch/38 projectiles, 80 percent of which were proximity fused, in addition to 540 rounds of 40-mm

and 1,342 of 20-mm ammunition. All three calibers of antiaircraft weapons scored hits. One *Alabama* sailor, Seaman 1st Class Harold George Olson of Minneapolis, Minnesota, was washed overboard during the action. He was rescued a short time later by the destroyer *Morrison* (DD-560) and returned to *Alabama* on the 16th.

Since the invasion of Leyte was nearly at hand, the task force turned south to assume positions east of the Philippines. As carrier aircraft assaulted the Visayas (the central Philippine Islands), *Alabama* stood ready to repel air attacks or join a surface action, but neither was forthcoming. She was ordered to return to Ulithi on 24 October but was almost immediately recalled.

THE BATTLE OF LEYTE GULF

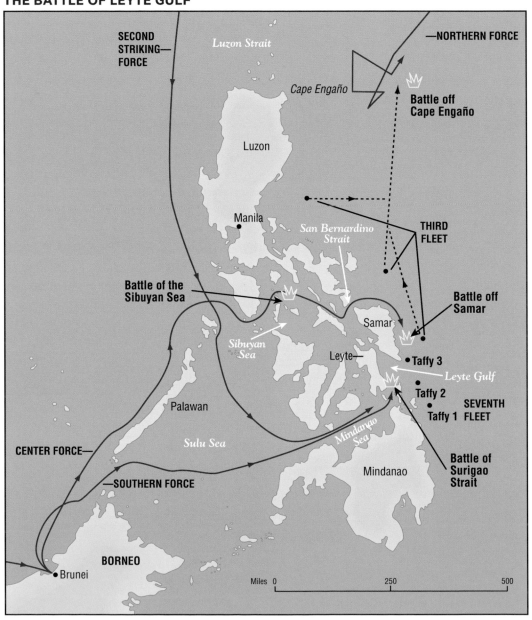

(Kelly Oaks)

UNITED STATES NAVAL INSTITUTE

The Battle of Surigao Strait was developing—a large element of the Japanese fleet was attempting to strike at the Leyte landings from the south. Before that battle was under way, *Alabama* received yet another change of orders, this time to join the Third Fleet off Cape Engaño (the northeastern tip of Luzon) for action against enemy forces believed to be there.

This move to Cape Engaño was exactly what the Japanese naval leadership had hoped for. Counting on Halsey's reputation as a hard charger, the Japanese had lured him there, using as bait their aircraft carriers, which by then had hardly any combat-ready aircraft. By sacrificing the impotent carriers, the Japanese could draw Halsey's fleet (including *Alabama* and the other fast battleships) away from a Japanese force that would be exiting the San Bernardino Strait north of the island of Samar. This force, including the massive Japanese battleship *Yamato*, would, if successful, swoop down on vulnerable U.S. transport and supply ships at Leyte Gulf and destroy them. It was only due to the extraordinary and selfless courage of the destroyers, destroyer escorts, and escort carriers of "Taffy 3," the unit that had been left behind and exposed by Halsey's withdrawal, were the Japanese beaten back at this, the Battle off Samar.

Meanwhile, at Cape Engaño with Task Force 34, which included five fast battleships, *Alabama* sounded General Quarters at 0520 on 25 October for imminent surface action. Had such an engagement occurred, it would have been the first of the war for her. Just as *Alabama* was about to close on Japanese ships reported to be only 50 miles distant and perhaps use her main batteries against surface vessels for what would have been the only time in the war, her orders were changed once again. A pointed query from Admiral Nimitz (see "The Misuse of the Fast Battleship in World War II" on page 16) had prompted Halsey to send the battleship force back to the San Bernardino Strait. Neither *Alabama* nor any other of the ships of this group arrived in time to catch the now-withdrawing Japanese. Her best chance to engage her 16-inch/45 guns against enemy ships had been narrowly lost off Cape Engaño, and now she had missed a second opportunity in the San Bernardino Strait.

Alabama remained with the carriers to the east of the central Philippines as they struck targets there until 28 October. She returned, as she had been originally ordered to do on 24 October, to Ulithi, reaching the atoll on 30 October. Her next action came on 5 and 6 November 1944, supporting carriers attacking northern

Luzon Island as part of Task Force 38 under Admiral John S. McCain Sr. on board the carrier *Wasp* (CV-18). Once again the carriers moved to attack the Visayas on 11 November, before returning to Luzon on the 13th and 19th. *Alabama* put up air-defense fire on 19 November at 8,300 yards, expending 82 rounds from her 5-inch/38 mounts using both standard Mark 18 fuses and Mark 32 proximity fuses. However, the fire was without apparent effect.

On 23 November 1944, *Alabama* was detached from Task Force 38 and returned yet again to Ulithi to be resupplied, reaching the atoll on 24 November and anchoring there for a week. She stood out on 1 December with the newly formed Task Group 38.5. Over the next few days she conducted main-battery and antiaircraft firing exercises as the task group steamed to an area about 150 miles north of Ulithi. By 14 December, *Alabama* and Task Force 38 were once again off the east coast of Luzon to strike Japanese positions there, in preparation for MacArthur's invasion of the island, now scheduled for mid-January 1945. As *Alabama* was taking part in refueling operations on 18 December 1944, the weather worsened dramatically. She and the other ships of Task Force 38 were about to be engulfed by a typhoon that would cost hundreds of lives (see "Typhoons" on page 68).

BATTLE STAR 8: OKINAWA GUNTO (OKINAWAN ISLANDS), MAY–JUNE 1945

Just after the typhoon of December 1944, *Alabama* received orders to proceed via Pearl Harbor to Puget Sound Navy Yard in Washington State. She would remain there from 12 January to 17 March 1945. This was her first full-scale refurbishment since commissioning in August 1942. Previous visits to navy yards at Norfolk (August 1943) and Pearl Harbor (January 1944) had been brief. The length of the stay at Puget Sound enabled many of the crew to be given leaves long enough to travel across the country and visit their families.

On 14 March, just days before standing out from Puget Sound, *Alabama* lost a crew member to an accident. Seaman 2nd Class Mann Woodfield Roberson Jr., of Mount Vernon, Indiana, accidentally stepped off the forward end of a lighter that was bringing supplies to *Alabama*. He did not resurface, and a search failed to locate him. His body was recovered a month later.

Upon exiting Puget Sound, *Alabama* steamed for the Los Angeles area to begin a testing period after its overhaul. The ship anchored at San Pedro (the port of Los Angeles) and conducted exercises in the vicinity of San Clemente Island. She fired 233 rounds from her refurbished main batteries, 1,429 from her 5-inch mounts, 6,424 rounds of 40-mm ammunition, and 30,600 rounds of 20-mm.

On 4 April 1945, *Alabama* set a new course westward for Pearl Harbor, participating in air attack exercises en route. On 10 April she moored there, staying until 18 April. While in the Hawaiian Islands, *Alabama* went to sea for further air-defense exercises, expending more 5-inch, 40-mm, and 20-mm rounds. On 14 April, the crew stopped for five minutes of silence to honor the memory of President Franklin Roosevelt, who had died on 12 April and whose funeral in Washington, DC, was held that day. The ship held a separate funeral service on board for Roosevelt on 15 April, the day the president was buried in Hyde Park, New York.

Repaired and renewed and manned by a crew whose gunnery abilities had been honed by frequent practice, *Alabama* left for the western Pacific on 18 April, arriving at the fleet anchorage at Ulithi Atoll, some 4,200 miles south-southwest of Pearl Harbor, on the 28 April. By this time the Battle of Okinawa,

for which she was headed, had been under way for four weeks.

Okinawa is the largest island in a group the United States referred to as the Ryukyu Islands. These islands lie about halfway between Kyushu, the southernmost large "home island" of Japan, and the Japanese-held island of Formosa. If the United States wanted to proceed with an invasion of the home islands in 1945, it would have to neutralize significant air bases on Okinawa and also isolate strongholds on Formosa and in mainland China. Thus the capture of Okinawa was essential, and possession of its air bases would allow concentrated air assaults on Japan prior to the invasion of Kyushu.

The era of the kamikaze suicide attack on U.S. and Allied shipping had commenced in earnest during the Battle of Leyte Gulf the previous fall. It would reach its peak during the Battle of Okinawa, near which hundreds of vulnerable warships were gathered to support the soldiers and Marines ashore, who had begun landing on 1 April. *Alabama*'s antiaircraft weapons would receive a full test in the most arduous of circumstances as she screened U.S. carriers whose fighters were attempting both to wipe out Japanese air power and intercept kamikaze pilots before they could reach U.S. warships.

USS *Enterprise* (CV-6) hit by a kamikaze while being screened by *Alabama*, 14 May 1945. (NARA)

From 9 May to 28 May 1945 *Alabama* operated as part of Admiral Mitscher's Task Force 58, the carrier USS *Enterprise* serving as his flagship. *Alabama* would be transferred to different task groups and task units as developments warranted. On 14 May, in Task Group 58.3, she shot at four of six planes that made it past the combat air patrol, downing two and assisting in the downing of a third. However, for the first time during the war, a carrier being screened by *Alabama* was damaged by air attack. At 0657 on 14 May observers on *Alabama* saw a Japanese Zero fighter dive out of low, heavy cloud cover and strike *Enterprise* at her forward elevator. For some reason, no enemy planes had been detected by radar within 15 miles.

At 0804 that same busy morning, *Alabama*'s 40-mm and 20-mm guns shot down a Zero 1,300 yards off her starboard beam. At 0813, a Zero in a shallow dive was taken under fire by the 5-inch, 40-mm, and 20-mm guns; it was struck and spun slowly into the sea about 2,600 yards away. Just three minutes later a 5-inch round with a VT fuse fired from *Alabama* helped down a third Zero.

Later that month, as an element of Task Group 38.1 (again in Admiral Halsey's Third Fleet), *Alabama* participated in further strikes on Kyushu but this time encountered no enemy forces. After enduring her second typhoon in six months (see "Typhoons" on page 68), she took part in the bombardment on 10 June 1945 of the island of Minami Daito Jima. This island, slightly more than 200 miles east of Okinawa, received 81 rounds from *Alabama*'s main battery and 70 from her 5-inch secondary battery.

Alabama thereupon steamed with her task group southwest toward the Philippines, specifically for San Pedro Bay in Leyte Gulf. On the way she conducted more antiaircraft live-fire exercises and participated in torpedo-attack drills with other ships of the group.

BATTLE STAR 9: OPERATIONS AGAINST JAPAN, JULY–AUGUST 1945

Alabama arrived at San Pedro Bay in Leyte Gulf on 13 June 1945 and spent nearly the next three weeks resupplying and otherwise preparing for operations against the Japanese home islands under Admiral Halsey on board USS *Missouri*. She engaged in routine firing practice for all her guns and took on abundant stocks of new ammunition for the next phase of her war.

On 1 July 1945 the Third Fleet, organized as Task Force 38 and commanded by Admiral McCain, got under way and headed around Samar Island and to the northeast. It took a roundabout path between Iwo Jima and Saipan before bending back toward the island of Honshu, on which Tokyo is located. The ships, *Alabama* among them, continued tactical exercises, including target practice at sleeves towed by friendly aircraft and at radio-controlled drones known as TDDs (Target Drone, Denny).

On 10 July, *Alabama* was 140 miles from the coast of Honshu when the carriers she was screening launched their attacks against targets in the Tokyo industrial area. These attacks did not produce a Japanese aerial or naval counterstrike. When the raids were complete,

THE LOCATIONS OF THE NINE BATTLE STARS WON IN WORLD WAR II

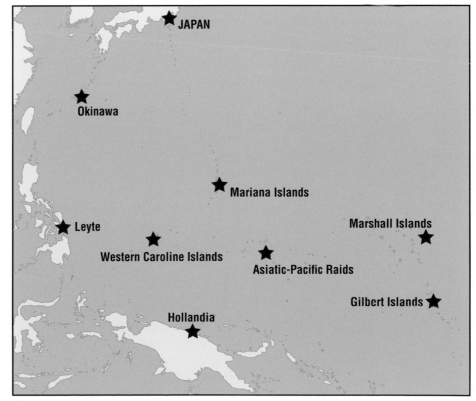

(Kelly Oaks)

the formation steamed to the north for attacks on the northernmost part of Honshu and on the island of Hokkaido. *Alabama* stood ready to help fend off challenges from the air, but none developed. The carrier planes too met little resistance. *Alabama*'s greatest service thus far in the operation was as a floating gas station: several destroyers received fuel oil from the battleship.

Alabama's formation turned south again down the coast of Honshu to an area near Hitachi, which it reached late on the evening of 17 July. It was now the turn of the battleships. As part of Task Unit 34.8.2, *Alabama* fired 271 rounds of 16-inch/45-caliber high-capacity ammunition at that heavily industrialized area. She then remained between Iwo Jima and Honshu, refueling destroyers and being refueled herself by oilers. The carriers continued to strike Japan, and still no airplanes sortied to attack this formation.

It is likely *Alabama* and the ships she screened would have continued in this way for months, adding to the mounting pressure on the leaders of a badly weakened Japan to surrender prior to a U.S.-led invasion. Other elements of that pressure are well known. The Soviet Union fulfilled a previous agreement with the Allies and declared war against Japan on 9 August. Until that day, Japan's leaders had been hoping the Soviets, who had resisted all efforts to pull them into the war against Japan while Germany was still fighting, might act as an intermediary to get better terms in peace negotiations than they might otherwise expect. A final element was, of course, the dropping of two atomic bombs on Japan, on 6 August (Hiroshima) and 9 August (Nagasaki). Even so, it was only by the personal intervention of Hirohito, emperor of Japan, that the government finally moved to sue for peace on Allied terms—provided they could keep the emperor, a deal that was accepted by President Harry Truman. On 15 August the sailors on board *Alabama* learned that offensive combat operations were to cease immediately, pending the formal surrender ceremony.

There had been one last sad duty for *Alabama*'s medical staff. On 9 August, during the carrier strikes against Japan, the destroyer *Borie* was hit by one of the last successful kamikaze attacks. *Alabama* transferred a physician and hospital corpsmen to *Borie* to assist the destroyer, which had only limited ability to care for casualties and was overwhelmed by

the carnage caused by the kamikaze, a Val bomber. Thirty-five sailors had died, 13 were missing, and 34 were seriously wounded, necessitating the call for assistance from far-better-equipped *Alabama*. The *Alabama* personnel were transferred by bosun's chair to the destroyer *Ault* and ultimately by the same method to *Borie*. They administered plasma, splinted broken bones, bandaged wounds, and prepared the dead for burial at sea the next day. After *Borie* rendezvoused with the hospital ship *Rescue* (AH-18) the *Alabama* men were returned to their ship.

After 15 August, *Alabama* remained well off the eastern coast of Honshu, fueling destroyers and conducting firing practice. In the coming days she would support carriers launching missions to locate Allied prisoners of war and demonstrate U.S. force in the skies over Japan. She was well outside Tokyo Bay on 2 September 1945 when Halsey, Nimitz, MacArthur, and delegations from many Allied nations gathered on board the battleship *Missouri* for the formal signing of the terms of surrender by representatives of the Japanese government. *Alabama* entered Tokyo Bay on 5 September, anchored, and granted some of her men liberty ashore for sightseeing. Meanwhile, like every other U.S. ship, *Alabama* began planning for discharging men who were eligible and transporting her crew and others back to the United States as soon as conditions warranted.

POSTWAR, SEPTEMBER 1945–JUNE 1962

Alabama remained in Tokyo Bay until 19 September 1945. Her next role was vital, but it was not in combat. She participated in Operation Magic Carpet, which transported men back to the United States for discharge from service. After embarking Magic Carpet men in Tokyo Bay, she steamed for Buckner Bay, Okinawa, and took on more on 23 September. She got under way from Okinawa for Pearl Harbor on 24 September, arriving on 4 October. The only notable activity for her crew during the entire voyage was some antiaircraft practice firing. On 9 October she got under way for San Francisco and at 1250 on 15 October passed under the Golden Gate Bridge, welcomed by hundreds who lined the bridge above. She held an open house for 9,000 of the citizens of the San Francisco area on Navy Day, 27 October, serving lemonade, chicken, and cookies.

Alabama steamed from San Francisco on 29 October 1945, experiencing on the way to San Pedro yet another tragedy unrelated to combat. Chief Boatswain's Mate Charlie Arnold Bray, of Shiloh Township, North Carolina, was discovered to be missing during rough seas and high winds that met the ship when she reached the open waters outside San Francisco Bay. He was presumed to have fallen overboard and drowned.

Alabama reached San Pedro on 31 October 1945 and remained for the rest of 1945, her wartime duties fully at an end. She next departed on 27 February 1946 for Puget Sound Naval Shipyard, where she would undergo an inactivation overhaul. She was decommissioned on 9 January 1947 and became part of the Bremerton Group of the U.S. Pacific Reserve Fleet until stricken from the Naval Vessel Register on 1 June 1962.

Alabama's home from 1947 to 1964, at the berthing area for the reserve fleet at Puget Sound, Washington. (NARA)

ALABAMA AS A MUSEUM

THE MUSEUM SHIP ERA IN MOBILE, 1965 TO THE PRESENT

In 1994 Jimmy Morris, a Mobile, Alabama, resident, recounted to his hometown newspaper, the *Register*, what had by then become an oft-told local story (with some variation in its precise details). In 1962, while an employee of the Mobile Chamber of Commerce, he had stopped by the offices of the newspaper. As a former "radio man," all things newsy interested him, and he walked over to the teletype machine to see the latest stories from around the world appear before his eyes. A brief piece he read on the machine startled him: the U.S. Navy planned to scrap four World War II battleships. One of the four was USS *Alabama*, then berthed at Bremerton, Washington. Indeed, a United Press International bulletin published in newspapers on 2 May 1962 noted that the ships "would be scrapped as obsolete and unfit."

According to a slightly longer story that appeared in the Birmingham *News* that same day, the Secretary of the Navy, Fred Korth, had informed Congress that the states for which the ships were named would be notified about the possibility of transferring certain memorabilia from the battleships to them before they were scrapped.

But some who were interested in such matters knew there was another model, pioneered by the states of Texas and North Carolina: acquiring the ships from the federal government and moving them to ports in their namesake states for continued service as museums. In 1948, USS *Texas* had entered her second life near Houston, and as recently as 1962 USS *North Carolina* had opened to the public as a museum in Wilmington.

As the state of Alabama's port city on a bay in the Gulf of Mexico, Mobile would be the natural place to bring *Alabama* if she could be saved from the ship-breaking yard. Morris contacted Stephens G. Croom, the chairman of the Chamber of Commerce's Historic Site Preservation Committee, to see what could be done. Croom put his committee behind an effort to bring *Alabama* to Mobile as a museum and memorial to all Alabama soldiers, sailors, airmen, and Marines from all wars. He asked Henri M. Aldridge, an attorney with International Paper Company, to lead the effort.

The committee members contacted their state legislators and the governor of Alabama, James Patterson, seeking their assistance. While the state officials were supportive, the estimates to bring *Alabama* to Mobile and establish a museum and memorial were in the range of a million dollars, a large sum for such an endeavor at the time. Private fundraising would have to cover most of the cost, although the state helped by providing the site for the memorial for one dollar, and the federal government too, by waiving, through an act of Congress, $15,000 in transit fees for the Panama Canal, then controlled by the United States.

Fundraising involved such measures as encouraging the schoolchildren of Alabama to contribute pennies, nickels, and dimes (which added up to a not-insignificant $78,245.26 by September 1964). An "Alabama Navy" was created, in which contributors could attain higher "ranks" with larger donations for the battleship: "rear admiral" cost $100; "vice admiral," $500; and "admiral," $1,000. By that same September, there were 1,741 rear admirals, 55 vice admirals, and 81 admirals. The largest single expense was over $400,000 to dredge a 32-foot-deep channel from the existing Mobile Bay ship channel two miles to the site selected for what was to become Battleship Park.

Although only three-quarters of the required amount had been raised by mid-1964, when it was time to take possession of *Alabama* from the Navy or lose the opportunity, the newly formed Battleship *Alabama* Commission borrowed the remainder. The state of Alabama took title to the vessel in Bremerton on 11 June 1964, and the ship was formally handed over on 6 July. The Navy retained the right to reclaim the ship in an emergency, and it has removed some parts and equipment over the decades to be used on ships still in service.

Some consideration had been given to firing up *Alabama*'s boilers again and steaming her to Mobile under her own power. In the end, it was deemed less expensive and easier to tow her, although the cost even of towing such a large ship 5,600 miles was daunting, as was the effort involved. The sum required was nearly $160,000, and the job was not only an arduous but a tragic one for the towing company, the Red Stack Line of San Francisco. On 22 July 1964, after *Alabama*'s four propellers had been removed and stored on her deck, two tugs, *Sea Lion* and *Sea Ranger*, began towing the newest museum ship out of Puget Sound at a speed of five knots. As the flotilla approached the Panama Canal on 22 August, *Sea Lion* capsized and sank, with the loss of the first mate, Ira Herman Goltry, 55, of Long Beach, California. Another tug, *Margaret Walsh*, was sent from Mobile to take *Sea Lion*'s place.

After carefully passing through the locks of the canal, with less than one foot to spare on each side of their tow, the tugs moved into the Caribbean, only to confront a challenge typical for late summer—

USS *Alabama* being towed through Puget Sound, Washington, at the start of its final voyage to Mobile, Alabama, September 1964. (NHHC)

hurricanes. Storms named Cleo and Dora made the Gulf of Mexico a dangerous place that August and September, and progress toward Mobile was halted so as not to involve *Alabama*, which had survived the western Pacific typhoons of 1944 and 1945, in yet another tropical cyclone, this time unable to maneuver on her own. Thus she arrived at Mobile four days later than planned, on 14 September 1964, and was moored in a prominent but temporary spot just south of downtown Mobile until the dredging of the path to her new home was complete. The citizens of the city could (and did) come to water's edge to gawk at the ship destined to become a permanent part of their skyline.

With the channel dredged, *Alabama* was towed to her new and permanent coordinates of 30° 40" 55' N, 88° 00" 52' W. Earth was filled in around her, and a visitor's center and parking lot constructed as the first part of an elaborate plan for the state's memorial to its veterans. Governor George C. Wallace spoke at the dedication and opening ceremony on 9 January 1965, and the first of millions of visitors boarded the ship.

Over the decades the park added outdoor displays of aircraft, naval guns, tanks and other armored vehicles, a *Gato*-class submarine from World War II (USS *Drum*, SS-228), smaller boats, and ultimately a climate-controlled aircraft pavilion. Memorials form a key part of the park. They include monuments to the fallen and veterans of the Korean and Vietnam Wars; monuments dedicated to the U.S. Coast Guard and those who fell in the attacks of September 11, 2001; and a memorial to military service dogs. *Alabama* and her park are located next to major east–west Interstate Highway 10, which means a steady stream of visitors from people crossing coastal Alabama to or from Florida.

Hurricanes continued to interfere with the smooth operation of the museum long after the two that had delayed *Alabama*'s arrival by four days in 1964. Hurricane Frederic in 1979 gave *Alabama* a reputation as the safest place to be in Mobile during a hurricane. Despite her location on the water, she was in fact wedged tightly into the bottom of Mobile Bay and was not moved by the rising waters of the hurricane,

Battleship Park in Mobile, Alabama, sometime after the late 1970s. USS *Drum* (SS-228) is moored to the left of *Alabama*. In 2001, *Drum* was moved ashore. (U.S. Naval Institute photo archive)

Memorial to war dogs at USS *Alabama* Battleship Memorial Park. (Daniel Rogers)

which made landfall just west of Mobile. The park's other attractions (and areas around Mobile) were not so fortunate, however: after the storm, *Drum* was found to have listed 10 degrees to starboard and been pushed 10 feet forward; the Kingfisher aircraft then on display on one of *Alabama*'s catapults had been tossed onto the fantail; and other aircraft and the gift shop had been heavily damaged.

When Hurricane Ivan roared up Mobile Bay in 2004, again *Alabama* fared well. But her luck ran out when huge Hurricane Katrina struck the Mississippi Gulf Coast in 2005. Those who had gathered in "the safest place in Mobile" greeted a tilted horizon when they emerged after the storm, as *Alabama* had been pushed so far toward land by a monster storm surge that she was listing eight degrees to port. The surge had also flooded the gift shop and damaged the aircraft pavilion. The park reopened soon, and the list was eventually corrected.

Storm damage was not the only peacetime enemy of *Alabama*. Decay that begins for all ships during their earliest days afloat had for the battleship been continuing unabated since 1942, often unchallenged due to the enormous expense of comprehensive repairs. By 1996, the Battleship Commission had been aware for several years of widespread small holes in the outermost

steel plating. Water that had been pumped into the holding tanks in the outer hull had been mixing with fuel oil that had been left in adjacent bunkers. The mixture was leaking from the ship into Mobile Bay. A boom was placed around the ship to contain the spill, and over 45,000 gallons of oil were pumped out. But many tens of thousands of gallons remained on board. To solve the problem, a cofferdam was constructed around the ship that would allow all water within to be removed. Workers then double-plated the hull above the point where the ship is embedded in mud and reflooded the cofferdam. The water can be pumped out again when needed, but the water normally inside the cofferdam still gives the impression of *Alabama* being afloat.

One other severe and ongoing challenge addressed by *Alabama*'s indefatigable team has been the wooden main deck, which has had to be patched with epoxy, fiberglass, plastic compounds, or covered with small pieces of sheet metal in many areas as its teak planks decayed owing to exposure to moisture and sunlight. In April 2022, the USS Alabama Battleship Commission announced that a new teak deck costing $8.5 million would be installed, ensuring that generations of future visitors would continue to experience the ship as her original "plank owners" did in 1942.

The ship has been the site of crew reunions over the decades. It has also been used for scout sleepovers, naturalization ceremonies, birthday parties, commissioning ceremonies of officers of the U.S. armed forces, and oaths of enlistment ceremonies for enlisted men and women. The huge and level grassy expanses near the ship have been the scene of sporting events and other large gatherings. Even Hollywood has come calling, using the battleship as a stand-in for USS *Iowa* (*War and Remembrance*), USS *Missouri* (*Under Siege*), and the cruiser USS *Indianapolis* (*USS* Indianapolis: *Men of Courage*).

One popular feature regularly offered by the Battleship *Alabama* Memorial Park is the Living History Crew. Historical reenactors, attired in Navy and Marine Corps uniforms appropriate to the World War II era, "fire" the 20-mm and 40-mm antiaircraft guns, sometimes (weather permitting) at "attacking" aircraft that swoop in over Mobile Bay and approach the ship. In reality, the Living History Crew is firing blanks, but the noise level and intensity are sufficient to give visitors something of a taste of *Alabama*'s main duty during World War II, protecting herself and her formations from enemy aircraft.

Alabama celebrated her 75th birthday in 2017. Fifty-two of those years had been spent in Mobile, and with continued loving care by her dedicated team, she will serve for many more as a monument to American naval ingenuity, manufacturing prowess, and technological innovation. Most importantly of all, she testifies each day to the courage of the thousands of crewmen from all portions of the United States who made her "The Mighty A."

The Living History Crew of USS *Alabama* re-enacts the firing of 20-mm guns over the starboard quarter, October 2019. (Daniel Rogers)

FROM USS *ALABAMA* BATTLESHIP MEMORIAL PARK

On 1 June 1962 Battleship *Alabama* was stricken from the naval register. The state of Alabama intervened, however, saving the ship from the breakers. BB-60 went on to serve a greater purpose. She arrived in Mobile, Alabama on 14 September 1964 after a journey of 5,600 nautical miles. Here, the battleship began her final mission: to honor the veterans who served aboard her, and serve as the anchor for a larger park that honors all of Alabama's veterans. Since opening to the public as a museum on 9 January 1965, the "Mighty A" has stood as a silent sentinel in Mobile Bay.

Alabama's long-life as a museum ship means she has been part of an elite group that has paved the way for others. Many hurdles have presented themselves over the years as the ship ages and her stewards have tried to find newer and more efficient ways to care for the vessel. One notable challenge was what to do with 1.7 million gallons of fuel oil. Another was the construction of a cofferdam, the first of its kind for a battleship, enabling restoration of the ship's hull.

The 21st century has been a renaissance for the entire museum ship field. New technologies and techniques have found their way to Battleship *Alabama*. 3D scanning of interior spaces and artifacts as well as the addition of 3D printing have made their way aboard. A YouTube channel has been launched that enables the public to experience on board exhibits from their own homes. Cutting-edge holograms and motion-activated sounds make visitors feel as if they have walked back in time to 1945. That doesn't mean the tried and true methods of the U.S. Navy aren't still alive and well.

Needle scalers can still be heard regularly aboard the sleeping warship. Fresh paint can be smelled throughout as the staff and volunteers work tirelessly to keep her looking ready for sea duty. Compartments are constantly under restoration and preservation, artifacts are being displayed to make it look as if the crew just stepped away. Exhibits are being created and revamped to keep information fresh and interactive for the next generation. Today the Mighty A is in the process of receiving a new teak deck, the largest and most ambitious preservation project the ship has undertaken in almost twenty years. The USS *Alabama* Battleship Commission is committed to the ongoing preservation and maintenance of Battleship *Alabama*, ensuring her presence for future generations.

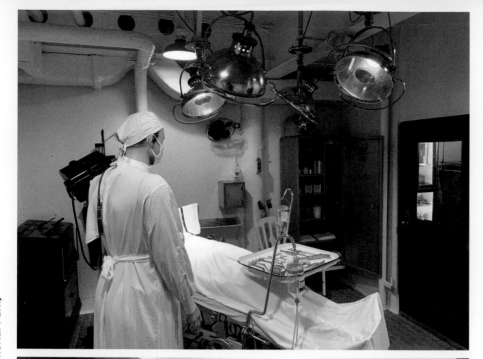

The Operating Room restoration was completed in 2016. *Alabama*, unlike many other ships of the time, had a tile floor installed in several areas within Sick Bay.

The Dispensary was home to pharmacist mates and again shows *Alabama's* unique tile deck. This area was restored through staff and volunteer efforts.

The outboard view of the Dispensary. Medical stores can be seen just above the fuel tanks of the USS *Alabama*.

What does every small floating city need? A Post Office. This compartment was completely restored in 2017, simultaneously with the construction of the Dive Exhibit.

USS *Alabama's* Chart House was restored from 2016–2017. This photo shows the port side of the compartment.

The Deep South Amateur Radio Club has been involved with the restoration of Radio Central, Radio 2, and Main Communication for the last two years. Proper paint colors have been applied to both the compartment and the furniture.

This Mk. V dive suit was conserved and placed in this newly constructed display in 2017. Divers, part of R Division, were needed to help inspect the hull below the waterline, as well as effect smaller repairs.

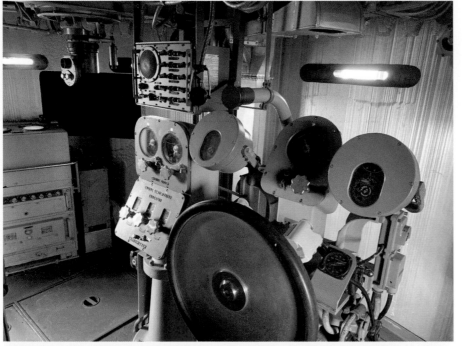

The Conning Station of the battleship. The crew referred to it as the "Battle Bridge." The armor is 16 inches thick in this location. This space was restored from 2016–2017.

Progress on the deck includes carefully sealing the new teak deck. Features of the original deck have been recreated, such as around this 20-mm gun mount.

WORLD OF WARSHIPS

World of Warships is a free-to-play, naval warfare–themed, massively multiplayer online game produced and published by Wargaming. Like their other games, *World of Tanks* (WoT) and *World of Warplanes* (WoWP), players take control of historic vehicles to battle others in player-versus-player or play ccooperatively against bots or in an advanced player-versus-environment (PvE) battle mode. *World of Warships* (WoWs) was originally released for PC in 2015; the PlayStation 4 and Xbox One console versions, titled *World of Warships: Legends*, followed in 2019, and it was released on the PlayStation 5 and Xbox Series X/S in April 2021.

Developed by Lesta Studios in St. Petersburg, Russia, *World of Warships* (PC) currently has more than 44 million registered players—playing on five main servers across the globe. More than 500 dedicated staff members work on a four-week update cycle to bring new features, ships, and mechanics to the game—keeping gameplay fresh and inviting to new players. The game features more than 400 ships, spread across 12 different in-game nations. Ships are designed based on historical documents and actual blueprints from the first half of the 20th century, and it takes from two to six man-months on average to create each of these ships. There are more than 20 ports to choose from, and 10 of them are re-created based on historical harbors and port towns.

There are four different ship classes: destroyers, cruisers, battleships, and aircraft carriers, with each class offering a different gameplay experience. Submarines have been in testing cycles since 2018, and based on testing results and player feedback, they have undergone significant changes that should allow them to launch as the fifth class in the near future. Ships are arranged in tiers between I and X, and players must progress through ship classes and tiers to reach tier X. Ships of tier X represent the pinnacle of naval engineering from World War II and the early Cold War era. Each warship needs a naval commander to lead it into the battle. There are many commanders

to choose from in *World of Warships*, including more than 10 iconic historical figures. In *World of Warships* players can battle on more than 40 maps. There are seven different permanent or seasonal Battle Types to choose from: Co-op Battles, Random Battles, Ranked Battles, Clan Battles, Brawls, Scenarios, and Training. From time-to-time additional Event battles are held. Additionally, within Battle Types there are four different Battle Modes available: Standard, Domination, Epicenter, and Arms Race.

Alabama made her *World of Warships* PC debut at the end of 2017. She shares many characteristics with her tech tree counterpart, *North Carolina*. *Massachusetts* made her *World of Warships* PC debut in June of 2018, and since then she has become a fan favorite. Her decent armor, speed, and guns make her a formidable opponent. In game, her guns are less accurate than her sister, *Alabama*, but it is her dual-purpose 5-inch battery that really shines. *Massachusetts* has some of the best secondary battery performance in the game—enemy ships really need to think twice before approaching her. *Alabama* and *Massachusetts* have since been removed from sale on PC, but *Massachusetts* is still available in *World of Warships: Legends*—on console. See the code on the back for your opportunity to play *Massachusetts* in *World of Warships* today.

Developed by the team behind *World of Warships* for PC, *World of Warships: Legends* is a completely new entry in Wargaming's flagship nautical franchise that takes full advantage of the power and capabilities of home consoles. *World of Warships: Legends* brings the online naval action loved by millions to home consoles for the very first time, alongside a host of content and features exclusive to the console experience. *World of Warships: Legends* is now available for download from the PlayStation® Store and Microsoft Store. Players can now wage wars across a variety of maps, in numerous warships, and enjoy stunning oceanic vistas with glorious HDR support on PlayStation®4 and Xbox One X. Full 4K support is available on PlayStation®4 Pro, PlayStation®5, and Xbox One X too! *Legends* also supports standard high-def on PlayStation®4 and Xbox One, with more intriguing graphics on the horizon.

Wargaming proudly supports various charitable causes that members of the gaming and history community care deeply about. Supporting veterans and servicemembers: Operation Lifeboat (2020) raised $150,000 USD for Stack Up's mental health awareness helpline; Remembrance charity drive

(2020) raised $45,000 USD for Help for Heroes, which supports UK veterans and servicemembers; and Project Valor (2017) saw WoWS, WoT, and WoWP collectively raise $75,000 USD for a veteran housing program. Preserving historical ship museums: *World of Warships*, in partnership with museums across the world to support the preservation of naval history and the education of the global community, raised $50,000 USD for the restoration of USS *Batfish* (2019) and $400,000 USD for the restoration of USS *Texas* (2017). Finally, supporting the local community: a 24-hour charity livestream (2019) raised $43,000 USD for the Save the Children organization, and also raised $78,000 USD for Team Rubicon and the victims of Hurricane Harvey in 2017.

The United States Naval Institute (USNI) has been a proud partner of *World of Warships* and Wargaming since December 2019. Wargaming has a made a commitment to naval history through various programs and events over the past years. It produces excellent video content with its *Naval Legends* series on YouTube, and hosts events on board museum ships where members of the gaming and naval history communities can get together and experience living history in person. *World of Warships* and Wargaming are also great sponsors of the Historic Naval Ships Association (HNSA). USNI thanks Wargaming and *World of Warships* for their continued support of the naval history community and their participation in this Naval History Special Edition. Please see the back cover for a special offer for *World of Warships* PC and *World of Warships: Legends*.

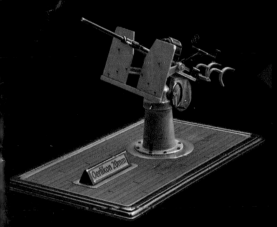

In 1940, during the war, the United States began looking for a replacement for the obsolete and weak Browning AA machine guns. The 20-mm automatic Oerlikon, significantly improved by that time, proved to be very useful. In 1941, production began in the United States, and soon the Oerlikons were mounted on almost every warship, from boats to battleships. USS *Alabama* carried 35 of these weapons during World War II.

The Mark 12 5-inch/38-cal gun would prove invaluable to the U.S. Navy in World War II. The MK 29 and 32 dual-purpose mounts were a highly efficient artillery system. A heavy-duty power drive and reliable mechanism ensured a fast horizontal and vertical aiming speed—perfect for use in the antiaircraft role. The mount had a nominal rate of fire of 15 shots per minute, but that could be increased for a short period of time, shooting up to 22 shells per minute. Each 5/38 shell weighed more than 50 lbs. USS *Alabama* was built with 10 MK 32 mounts, 5 per side.

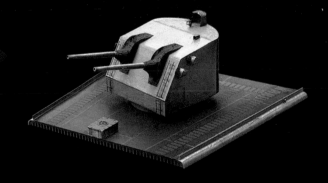

The 40-mm Bofors was produced in a variety of versions: with air and water cooling; in twin, quadruple, and single mounts; with manual aiming; and with power drive. More than ten thousand mounts were manufactured for the Navy and Coast Guard and more than twenty thousand for the Army, and around nine thousand were supplied to allied countries. USS *Alabama* was equipped with seven quad-mounted 40-mm Bofors during World War II.

NAVAL INSTITUTE PRESS

books you might also enjoy

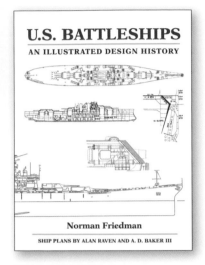

978-1-68247-758-8
Hardcover

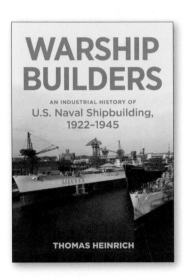

978-1-68247-537-9
Hardcover | 📱

978-1-68247-593-5
Hardcover | 📱

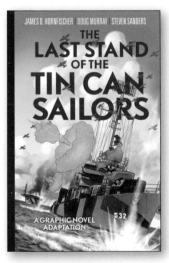

978-1-68247-338-2
Hardcover | 📱

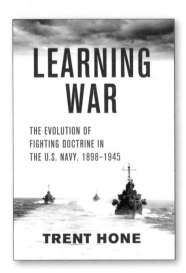

978-1-68247-836-3
Paperback

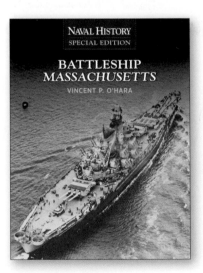

978-1-68247-635-2
Paperback

Members receive discounts on all books, see the website for details.

Available at www.usni.org/books

UNITED STATES NAVAL INSTITUTE